Douglas Hall holds doctorates in letters, philosophy and [illegible]
versity of L[illegible]
taught in th[illegible]
versity of Maryland.

THE TRINITY

STUDIEN UND TEXTE
ZUR GEISTESGESCHICHTE
DES MITTELALTERS

HERAUSGEGEBEN VON

Dr. ALBERT ZIMMERMANN

PROFESSOR AN DER UNIVERSITÄT KÖLN

BAND XXXIII

THE TRINITY

THE TRINITY

An Analysis of St. Thomas Aquinas'
Expositio *of the* De Trinitate *of*
Boethius

BY

DOUGLAS C. HALL

E.J. BRILL
LEIDEN • NEW YORK • KÖLN
1992

The paper in this book meets the guidelines for permanence and durability of the Committee on Production Guidelines for Book Longevity of the Council on Library Resources.

Library of Congress Cataloging-in-Publication Data

Hall, Douglas C.
   The Trinity : an analysis of St. Thomas Aquinas' "Expositio" of the "De Trinitate" of Boethius / by Douglas C. Hall.
      p.   cm. — (Studien und Texte zur Geistesgeschichte des Mittelalters. ISSN 0169-8125 ; Bd. 33)
   Includes bibliographical references and index.
   ISBN 9004096310 (alk. paper)
   1. Boethius, d. 524. De Trinitate.   2. Trinity—Early works to 18.00.   3. Thomas, Aquinas, Saint, 1225?-1274. Expositio super librum Boethii De Trinitate.   I. Title.   II. Series.
   BT110.H35   1992

92-10928
CIP

ISSN   0169-8125
ISBN   90 04 09631 0

PRINTED IN THE NETHERLANDS

CONTENTS

CHAPTER ONE

INTRODUCTION

Augustine, whom the distinguished Jaroslav Pelikan lauds as a "universal genius" and "almost certainly the greatest man who ever wrote Latin,"[1] and whose Trinitarian theology the brilliant Bernard Lonergan praises as "the high-water mark in Christian attempts to reach an understanding of the faith,"[2] labored for at least fifteen years on his monumental *De Trinitate*.[3] Writing to his friend, Bishop Aurelius of Carthage, Augustine remarked that he had begun the *De Trinitate* in his youth, but finished it as an old man.[4] And yet, while he made only a few changes in the text at the end of his life, it is clear that he was less than completely satisfied with it. As he brought his epoch-making masterpiece to a close, Augustine confessed:

> My words inadequately expressed the ideas, be they what they were, that I had formed about it in my mind, although even in my actual understanding of it I felt that I had made an attempt more than I had achieved success.[5]

Augustine, the theologian who most of all must be encountered in the outpouring of his self-revealing communication, concluded his painful struggle with Mystery in Trinitarian theology in a gasping psalm of lament:

---

[1] J. Pelikan, *The Christian Tradition: A History of the Development of Doctrine*, vol. 1: *The Emergence of the Catholic Tradition, 100-600* (Chicago: The University of Chicago Press, 1971), p. 292. For Pelikan, "Any theologian who could have written either the *Confessions* or the *City of God* or *On the Trinity* would have to be counted as a major figure in intellectual history. Augustine wrote them all, and vastly more" (p. 292).

[2] B. Lonergan, *Verbum: Word and Idea in Aquinas*, ed. D. Burrell (Notre Dame: University of Notre Dame Press, 1967), p. xiii.

[3] For G. Bardy, *Saint Augustin: L'homme et l'oeuvre*, 6th ed. (Paris: Desclée de Brouwer, 1946), pp. 338-341, the work may be dated 400-416. However for F. Glorie, "Augustinus, 'De Trinitate': Fontes - Chronologia," *Sacris Erudiri* 16 (1965), 203-255, the work was begun in 397 and finally completed in 412/413. For E. Hendrikx, "Le date de composition du 'De Trinitate' de saint Augustin," *L'année théologique augustinienne* 12 (1952), 305-316, it was begun in 399, with the final redaction being finished in 419. A longer period of composition is favored by A. Schindler, *Wort und Analogie in Augustins Trinitätslehre* (Tübingen: Mohr, 1965), who proposes the period 399-421.

[4] Augustine, *Epistula*, 174.

[5] Augustine, *De Trinitate*, Book 15, Chapter 25.

And you, O my soul, where do you find yourself to be, where do you lie down ... ? You recognize indeed that you are in that inn to which that Samaritan brought him whom he found half-dead from the many 'wounds' ... .[6]

If such was the fate of Augustine, should lesser mortals dare to gaze into such blinding, wounding Mystery?

The seminal project of the genius of Lonergan, *Verbum: Word and Idea in Aquinas*, overcame centuries of misinterpretation with boldly insightful yet historically grounded analyses, precisely in order to lay the groundwork for an understanding of the Trinitarian theology of Aquinas. At the end of Lonergan's monumental work, he expressed the view that if a completely genuine development of the thought of Aquinas could be accomplished, it would command in all the universities of the world the same admiration Aquinas himself received in the medieval University of Paris; yet the immediately following lament of Lonergan was that, "it remains that so sanguine an expectation has not yet been brought to birth."[7]

Perhaps anyone considering embarking on a project of Trinitarian theology would do well to first consider the statements of Augustine and Lonergan as serious words of warning. And perhaps anyone planning an analysis of the Trinitarian theology of Aquinas should first thoroughly ponder the fact that Aquinas' own, principal work combining reflections on theological methodology and Trinitarian theology, his *Expositio* of the *De Trinitate*, remained unfinished. Likewise, perhaps one should ponder the fact that Lonergan himself was unable to revise and finish his parallel project, *De Deo Trino*[8] before his death. But it may be that before one embarks on a project of Trinitarian theology, such warnings, and lessons from the historically factual "fate" which met previous attempts, cannot be appreciated.

In the entire history of Western Trinitarian theology, one of the most bold attempts to logically and philosophically penetrate the *De Trinitate* of Augustine was, precisely, the *Trinitas unus Deus ac non tres Dii (The Trinity is One God and not Three Gods)* - also known as the *De Trinitate* - of Boethius; and the greatest medieval analysis of this theological tractate of Boethius was that of Thomas Aquinas. The purpose of the present study is to disclose the theological methodologies and the contents of this Boethian tractate and the *Expositio* of Aquinas.

---

[6]   Ibid., Chapter 26.
[7]   Lonergan, *Verbum: Word and Idea in Aquinas*, p. 220.
[8]   B. Lonergan, *De Deo Trino*, 2 vols. (Rome: Gregorian University Press, 1964).

Thematics in the 20th-Century Recovery and Expansion of Aquinas

Although Aquinas was a philosopher and theologian of the 13th century, it may well be said that it is only in the 20th century that many central aspects of his thought are beginning to be grasped in the breadth of their synthetic significance. It is only in the late 20th century that the critical editions of the works of Aquinas are finally within sight of completion,[9] and the massive *Index Thomisticus*,[10] even though not completely based on critical texts, makes possible a depth of detail in textual analysis that was previously unattainable. Furthermore, advances in classical scholarship during the 19th and 20th centuries have enabled a far more accurate understanding of the Platonic, Aristotelian, Neoplatonic and Augustinian, as well as Arab-Aristotelian heritage bequeathed to Aquinas; and medieval studies have provided a fuller context to the questions and methodologies both of Aquinas himself and of the 13th century in general. Thus in many ways the late 20th century is witnessing a renewed exploration of the thought of Aquinas, finally freed from some of the limitations of previous traditions, which only dwarfed and dimmed his brilliance. A major need of late-20th-century thomistic studies is now an integration of thematics which have emerged in mid-20th-century scholarship.

Rather than speak of "Thomism" or even "schools of thomistic thought," it is more accurate at the end of the 20th century to speak of "thematics of thomistic interpretation."

Three fundamental thematics have emerged in 20th-century thomistic hermeneutics which are of critical and central significance both for an accurate understanding of Aquinas' methodology and his theology of the Trinity. These movements are more properly termed "thematics" since they are not clearly defined "schools" as much as they are various theorists united under a central theme while still differing on particular points of interpretation. To analyze and refine the contributions of these three main currents, and to cast them into a mutually correcting synthesis, is one of the major tasks facing late-20th-century thomists. These three currents of interpretation may be characterized as: participationist, transcendental, and analogical. They all share an historico-critical methodology.

---

[9]   See P.-M. de Contenson, "Documents sur les premiéres annés de la Commission Léonine," *St. Thomas Aquinas 1274-1974: Commemorative Studies*, 2 vols., ed. A. Maurer (Toronto: Pontifical Institute of Mediaeval Studies, 1974), vol. 2, pp. 331-388; "Principles, Methods, and Problems of the Critical Edition of the Works of St. Thomas as Presented in the Leonine Edition," *Tijdschrift voor Philosophie* 36 (1974), 342-364; C. Murphy, "All the Pope's Men: Putting Aquinas Together Again," *Harper's* (June 1979), pp. 45-64.

[10]   *Index Thomisticus: Sancti Thomae Aquinatis Operum Omnium Indices et Concordantiae*, ed. R. Busa (Stuttgart: F. Fromman Verlag, 1974-80).

The participationist stances of Fabro, Geiger, and Montagnes[11] have made it apparent that the originality of Aquinas' adaptations of Aristotle and his indebtedness to the Neoplatonic tradition were both far greater than ever conceived at the beginning of the thomistic revival in the 19th century. Aquinas actually provided a synthesis of Aristotle and Plotinian Neoplatonism, with a result that can at times be called an Aristotelianism specified by Platonism, and at times a fundamental Platonism specified by Aristotelianism.

The various "transcendental" thematics of Maréchal, Rahner, and Lonergan[12] have, in various ways, emphasized the dynamic structure of the human knower. The exact meaning of the "transcendental" is presented differently by Maréchal, Rahner, and Lonergan as their methodologies and purposes are often quite distinct; but the scope of their concern includes a resetting of questions raised by Kant, Heidegger and modern philosophy of science and bringing these to bear on thomistic epistemology.

One of Maréchal's fundamental theses was that Kant became a critical idealist because he was inconsistent in his own reflection on the *a priori* conditions of human knowledge.[13] For Maréchal, Kant forgot that the mind's act of knowing is dynamic, a motion toward an end, and that the only

[11]   C. Fabro, *La nozione metafisica di participazione secondo S. Tommaso d'Aquino* (Milano: Soc. Ed. Vita e Pensiero, 1939; 2nd ed. Torino: Soc. Ed. Internazionale, 1950; 3rd ed., 1963); *Partecipazione e causalità* (Torino: Soc. Ed. Internazionale, 1961); *Participation et causalité selon s. Thomas d'Aquin* (Louvain: Publications Universitaires, 1961); L.-B. Geiger, *La participation dans la philosophie de s. Thomas d'Aquin* (Paris: Vrin, 1942; 2nd ed., 1952); B. Montagnes, *La doctrine de l'analogie de l'être d'après s. Thomas d'Aquin* (Louvain: Publications Universitaires, 1963). Montagnes' work is of particular merit in its integration of participationist and analogical themes. L. de Raeymaeker was also one of the earliest writers to incorporate a greater stress on participation in general metaphysics; see his *Metaphysica Generalis*, 2nd ed. (Louvain: Warny, 1935); *De metaphysiek van het zijn* (Antwerpen: Standaard Boekhandel; Nijmegen: Dekker and Van der Vegt, 1944, 2nd Dutch ed., 1947). The first French edition of the same work, *Philosophie de l'être: Essai de synthèse métaphysique* (Louvain: Institut Supérieur de Philosophie, 1945), gave further expansion to the theme of participation, which was continued in the 2nd French edition (Louvain: Institut Supérieur de Philosophie, 1947) and in the English translation by Ziegelmeyer, *The Philosophy of Being: A Synthesis of Metaphysics* (London and St. Louis: Herder, 1966). A third French edition was also published (Louvain: Editions Nauwelaerts; Paris: Béatrice-Nauwelaerts, 1970). See also A. Gonzalez, *Ser y participación. Estudio sobre la cuarta via de Tomás de Aquino* (Pamplona: Eunsa, 1979); M. Sanchez Sorondo, *La gracia como participación de la naturaleza divina* (Buenos Aires-Letran-Salamanca: Universidades Pontificias, 1979).

[12]   J. Maréchal, *Le point de départ de la métaphysique. Leçons sur le développement historique et théorique du probléme de la connaissance* (Bruges: Beyaert; Louvain: Museum Lessianum, 4 vol., 1923-26; 3rd ed., Bruxelles: Editions Universelles; Paris: Desclée, 5 vol., 1944ff); K. Rahner, *Geist in Welt. Zur Metaphysik der endlichen Erkenntis bei Thomas von Aquin* (Innsbruck-Leipzig: Rausch, 1939; 2nd ed., rev. by J. Metz, Munich: Kösel-Verlag, 1957); *Spirit in the World*, trans. of 2nd ed. by Dych (New York: Herder and Herder, 1968); Lonergan, *Verbum: Word and Idea in Aquinas* and *Insight: A Study of Human Understanding* (New York: Philosophical Library, 1957).

[13]   See discussion in G. McCool, *Catholic Theology in the Nineteenth Century: The Quest for a Unitary Method* (New York: Seabury, 1977), pp. 255-257.

possible end of an intellectual movement, which transcends every limited object, is Unlimited Being. Thus in Maréchal, there is a confrontation between Aquinas and Kant in which the transcendental method of Kant is revised into a realistic metaphysics. The corrected inconsistency in Kant is synthesized with Aquinas, in that the *a priori* condition of possibility for every speculative judgement is the existence of Pure *Esse* as the term of the mind's dynamism. The idealism of Kant is corrected in Maréchal's observation that in every act of judgement a universal form must be united to a sensible singular and then the existence of this universal must be affirmed objectively: "it is." There is an extramental correlate of objective judgement.

Karl Rahner and Bernard Lonergan have unquestionably been the most influential transcendental thomists in the period after Vatican II. In ways unimaginable to Kleutgen,[14] both Rahner and Lonergan are descriptive phenomenologists in the sense that they attend to the dynamic process of knowing in its movement toward Infinite Being. Both are historico-critical thomists, receptive to theological pluralism and aware of the importance of conceptual frameworks, and yet they find in their phenomenological descriptions of human consciousness a basis for a defense against relativism. Both involve a thomistic view of analogy and participation, though in varying ways.

Parallel and complementary to the emergence of the participationist and transcendental interpretations, there was a revision of generally accepted notions of "analogy" in the philosophy of Aquinas. Here the studies of Klubertanz, Lyttkens, McInerny, Mondin, and Anderson have been of importance.[15] Klubertanz and Montagnes have sought to explicate the central link of participation and analogy. Fabro himself has stated that the exposition of Aquinas' doctrine of analogy is impossible without consideration of his notion of participation.[16] Geiger holds that the ontological foundation for

---

[14] J. Kleutgen, *Die Theologie der Vorzeit*, 2 vols. (Münster: Theissing, 1853, 1854); *Die Philosophie der Vorzeit vertheidigt*, 2nd ed. (Innsbruck: Rausch, 1878). See also discussion in McCool, *Catholic Theology in the Nineteenth Century*, and T. Hartley, *Thomistic Revival and the Modernist Era*. St. Michael's in Toronto Studies in Religion and Theology, Dissertation Series, 1 (Toronto: Institute of Christian Thought, University of St. Michael's College, 1971).

[15] G. Klubertanz, *St. Thomas Aquinas on Analogy: A Textual Analysis and Systematic Synthesis* (Chicago: Loyola University Press, 1960); H. Lyttkens, *The Analogy Between God and the World: An Investigation of Its Background and Interpretation of Its Use by Thomas of Aquino* (Uppsala: Almqvist and Wicksells, 1952); R. McInerny, *The Logic of Analogy: An Interpretation of St. Thomas* (The Hague: Martinus Nijhoff, 1961); *Studies in Analogy* (The Hague: Martinus Nijhoff, 1968); B. Mondin, *The Principle of Analogy in Protestant and Catholic Theology* (The Hague: Martinus Nijhoff, 1963); J. F. Anderson, *Reflections on the Analogy of Being* (The Hague: Martinus Nijhoff, 1967); B. Montagnes, *La doctrine de l'analogie de l'être d'après s. Thomas d'Aquin*. See also the integration of themes by M. Sciacca, "Riflessioni sui principi della metafisica tomista: l'esistenza e l'essenza; la creazione, la partecipazione e l'analogia," *Tommaso d'Aquino nel suo VII Centenario*, 9 vols. (Rome: Herder; Naples: d'Auria, 1975-1978), vol. 3, pp. 18-29.

[16] Fabro, *La nozione metafisica di participazione*, 2nd ed., p. 189, fn2.

analogy is to be found in participation.[17] For Hill, it is participation which is the basis of transcendental analogy in Aquinas.[18] For Montagnes, analogy is the very "semantics" of participation.[19]

And yet, while Fabro acknowledges with great insight the interconnection of participation and analogy, he has been quite persistent in his scathing criticism of the "transcendental school," represented in different ways by Maréchal, Rahner, and Lonergan, and has thus given the impression that no synthesis could be possible between his participationist view and the various stresses on the dynamism of the human intellect presented by the transcendentalists:

> By deriving the *actus essendi*, understood in the nominalistic sense of existence, from the act of judgement, the neoscholasticism of Maréchal and his school (Lotz, Rahner, Marc, Coreth, Brugger, Metz) has accepted the modern principle of immanence ... while Rahner takes his inspiration directly from the thematic of Heidegger's existential Kantianism, B. Lonergan (cf. *Insight, Verbum*) accepts his 'transcendental' directly from the *Kritik der reinen Vernunft*.[20]

But a close analysis of Fabro and the transcendentalists reveals that such a synthesis and mutual corrective is indeed possible. The scope of Fabro's rejection of such a possibility is, indeed, quite broad. In order to explore his criticism in depth one would need to specify exactly what is meant by "actus essendi," "nominalistic sense of existence," "act of judgement," "modern principle of immanence," the historically vague and questionably accurate term "Heidegger's existential Kantianism," and the, in fact, differing notions of the "transcendental" in Kant and Lonergan. It is not the case that either Rahner or Lonergan have a nominalistic sense of "existence" derived from judgement. Rather, the judgement of existence precisely reaches objectivity. The act of judgement is not the ultimate basis for existence, in a nominalistic sense, but merely the mental operation through which knowledge of existence is attained. Maréchal and Rahner certainly do have a principle of immanence, but although its status is not always clarified in the manner or to the extent

[17] Geiger, *La participation dans la philosophie de s. Thomas d'Aquin*, 2nd ed., p. 317, fn3.
[18] W. Hill, *Knowing the Unknown God* (New York: Philosophical Library, 1971), see esp. pp. 127-128.
[19] Montagnes, *La doctrine de l'analogie de l'être d'après s. Thomas d'Aquin*, esp. p. 10.
[20] C. Fabro, "The Intensive Hermeneutics of Thomistic Philosophy: The Notion of Participation," *The Review of Metaphysics* 27 (1974), 470, fn68. See also A. Maurer, *St. Thomas Aquinas: Faith, Reason, and Theology: Questions I-IV of his Commentary on the 'De Trinitate' of Boethius*. Medieval Sources In Translation, 32 (Toronto: Pontifical Institute of Medieval Studies, 1987), p. x, fn9, when he states that K. Rahner's, "approach to theology uses a transcendental method that owes more to Kant and the German idealists than to Thomas Aquinas."

that one would like, it is ultimately a participatory immanence and not an absolute immanence.[21]

Thus, a problem remains in the general literature: how can one further integrate the participationist, transcendental, and analogical thematics? More basically, how can one integrate the dialectical aspects in each of these thematics with the dialectical aspects in the others? Further, how is this of benefit both for theological methodology and, in particular, for a theology of the Trinity? The most apt loci for such a thematic integration and synthesis are twofold. The central aspect of the "natural" participation of the human subject is precisely in the structure of the agent intellect.[22] The central thematic of "supernatural participation" is precisely the human subject's entrance into what may be termed an "inter-personal subjectivity" with the divine Persons. Both the natural and the supernatural points of focus enable synthetic viewpoints. The particular, supernatural, theme of the human subject's entrance into an "inter-personal subjectivity" with the divine Persons is located within a general theology of the Trinity, the specific consideration of the "Gifts of the Holy Spirit," and the classical theme of the "Indwelling Trinity."

There is also another entrance into the integration of the fundamental thematics, i.e., via theological methodology. It can be found that both the proposed and the actually implemented methodology of Aquinas integrates the participationist, transcendental, and analogical methodologies, along with the rich dialectical interplays found in each.

The Re-Emergence of the Question of Method

As Nietzsche observed, "methods themselves are the most precious truths";[23] they are the most essential and the most difficult, and they are the ones

---

[21] Fabro's criticisms are not always accurate: G. Sala, whom Fabro cites as support for his criticism of Lonergan, in fact differs from Fabro's assessment of the matter. See G. Sala, *Das Apriori in der menschlichen Erkenntnis: eine Studie über Kants Kritik der reinen Vernunft und Lonergans Insight* (Meisenheim am Glan: Hain, 1971). See also Lonergan's own explicit and multiple criticisms of Kant in *Insight*.

[22] See our introductory treatment in "Lumen Intellectus Agentis: The Participationist-Transcendental Ground of Human Knowledge in the Philosophy of Thomas Aquinas," (Ph.L. dissertation, The Higher Institute of Philosophy, Katholieke Universiteit Leuven, 1983). The theme of the agent intellect precisely as a participation in Intellect Itself is present in Fabro, and it has been a foundational principle of the epistemological efforts of Maréchal, Rahner, and Lonergan, even though they may not have, in each instance, provided a close textual study of the topic or attempted a reconciliation of various interpretations. Our previous, introductory, investigation, sought to provide a textual and contextual analysis of Aquinas in a way that would show the synthetic and mutually corrective power of a participationist-transcendental interpretation.

[23] F. Nietzsche, cited by C. Boff, *Theology and Praxis: Epistemological Foundations* (Maryknoll, N.Y.: Orbis, 1987), p. 236, n23.

discovered last.[24] The question of method is *the* fundamental question in science and in art. The re-emergence of the question of method in contemporary theology is well known. It is actually the radical question of every era in the history of theology. That which in contemporary terms is addressed as a question of "method" is often merely a partial aspect of classical considerations in which the more global status, the "an sit" and "quid sit," of theology was treated before an inquiry was made "de modo." There is no need here to retrace the genesis and development of the 20th-century question of method. What is of note here is the particular re-emergence of questions on both the status of theology as envisioned by Aquinas, and the theological methods proposed and employed by Aquinas,[25] and the emergence of the question of pluralism in theological methodologies within the traditions of Roman Catholicism.[26] Given the literature to date, questions regarding the more global status of theology, as envisioned by Aquinas, as well as the proposed and actually implemented theological methodologies of Aquinas are still worthy of consideration. The most massive and detailed analysis to date of the theological methodology of Aquinas is that of Corbin, in his *Le chemin de la théologie chez Thomas d'Aquin* (1974). What Corbin proposes is a type of Hegelian analysis of the

---

[24] F. Nietzsche, *The Antichrist* in *Twilight of the Idols and the Antichrist* (Baltimore: Penguin, 1968), p. 182.

[25] See, for example, R. Garrigou-Lagrange, *De Deo Uno: Commentarium in Primam Partem S. Thomae* (Paris: Desclée de Brouwer et Cie, 1938); Y. Congar, "Théologie," *Dictionnaire de Théologie Catholique*, XV, 1, cc. 341-502; a revision of this article was trans. by Guthrie, *A History of Theology* (Garden City: Doubleday, 1968), see esp. pp. 69-143; J. Weisheipl, "The Meaning of 'Sacra Doctrina' in 'Summa Theologiae' I, q. 1," *The Thomist* 38 (1974), 49-80; P. Persson, "Le plan de la Somme théologique et la rapport Ratio-Revelatio," *Revue philosophique de Louvain* (1958), 545-572; *Sacra Doctrina: Reason and Revelation in Aquinas*, trans. MacKenzie (Philadelphia: Fortress Press, 1970); G. Van Ackeren, *Sacra Doctrina: The Subject of the First Question of the Summa Theologica of St. Thomas Aquinas* (Rome: Catholic Book Agency, 1952); T. Gilby, the 14 masterful appendices, which constitute most of the volume, *Summa Theologiae*, vol. 1: *Christian Theology*, trans. with Introduction, Notes, Appendices and Glossary by T. Gilby (New York: McGraw-Hill Book Company; London: Eyre and Ode, 1964) [The "Blackfriars Edition"], pp. 43-148, esp. "Appendix 2: The Method of the 'Summa,'" "Appendix 5: 'Sacra Doctrina,'" "Appendix 6: Theology as Science," "Appendix 9: Doctrinal Development," and "Appendix 10: The Dialectic of Love in the 'Summa,'"; T. O'Brien, "'Sacra Doctrina' Revisited: The Context of Medieval Education," *The Thomist* 41 (1977), 475-509; V. Preller, *Divine Science and the Science of God: A Reformulation of Thomas Aquinas* (Princeton: Princeton University Press, 1967); B. Lonergan, esp. the methodological sections of *De Deo Trino* and his *Method in Theology* (New York: Herder and Herder, 1972); E. Schillebeeckx, *Revelation and Theology*, vol. 1 (New York: Sheed and Ward, 1967); D. Tracy, *Blessed Rage for Order* (New York: Seabury, 1975); McCool, *Catholic Theology in the Nineteenth Century*, G. LaFont, *Structures et méthode dans la Somme Théologique de saint Thomas* (Paris: Desclée de Brouwer, 1960), and M. Corbin, *Le chemin de la théologie chez Thomas d'Aquin* (Paris: Beauchesne, 1974).

[26] Cf. International Theological Commission, "L'Unité de la foi et le pluralisme théologique," *La Civiltá Cattolica* (5 May 1973); also published in *La documentation catholique* (20 May 1973). See also G. McCool, *From Unity to Pluralism: The Internal Evolution of Thomism* (New York: Fordham University Press, 1989).

texts of Aquinas in their chronological order. What Corbin accomplishes is quite admirable, but actually more of a chronological comparison of the order in which Aquinas treats themes in his methodological works. Reactions to Corbin's work have often included protests from American readers that his "Hegelian" analysis is too cloudy, and protests from other readers that his conclusions are too Barthian. The point of importance here is that Corbin's work is quite significant, and a major influence on the present study; and yet the work does not resolve all the issues - certainly no work can! The present study will differ from Corbin in that it will be more "hegelian" and more "barthian" in dialectics. The present study will also differ from Corbin in that it will not only look at the methodological texts of Aquinas as such, but also examine the problem of "content" in his Trinitarian theology. The present study will additionally differ from Maurer, McInerny, and Klünker.[27]

The Re-Emergence of the Trinitarian Question

The "Trinitarian Question" concerns both what theology can understand of what the Trinity is In-Itself, and the significance of the Trinitarian mystery for theology and for Christian life. Insofar as the fundamental nature of the human subject is considered as "imago Dei," the Trinitarian question is also ultimately an anthropological question. Likewise, the "anthropological question," insofar as it is raised by faithed-human consciousness, is also ultimately, in economic terms, the "Trinitarian Question." Thus, it is only with an adequately developed Trinitarian theology that one can attempt an adequately developed theology of the human subject and the structure of human consciousness. Likewise, it is only with an adequately developed theological anthropology that one can attempt an adequate Trinitarian theology. Without both moments there is no possibility of an authentically

---

[27] Maurer's, "Introduction" in *Thomas Aquinas: Faith, Reason and Theology*, correctly sees dialectical elements (see, e.g., pp. xiv-xv, xx, xxii, xxviii) in faith and reason, but does not explicate the structure that results from these elements - a task which he also did not intend to undertake in his brief "Introduction." R. McInerny, *Boethius and Aquinas* (Washington, D.C.: The Catholic University of America Press, 1990) provides a basically helpful introduction, but does not refer to Corbin, Maurer or even Wippel. McInerny gives a flat reading which might be a useful introduction for the beginning student, although his primary thesis (p. xiv) is too simplistic. By comparison, the "Einführung" by W.-U. Klünker in *Thomas von Aquin: Über die Trinität: Eine Auslegung der gleichnamigen Schrift des Boethius in Librum Boethii de Trinitate Expositio*. Übersetzung und Erläuterungen von H. Lentz, mit einer Einführung von W.-U. Klünker (Stuttgart: Verlag Freies Geistesleben, 1988) is more nuanced on hermeneutical, epistemological, and methodological issues - though very brief. For a further discussion of methodological points, see our "Participated Trinitarian Relations: Dialectics of Method, Understanding, and Mystery in the Theology of St. Thomas Aquinas" (S.T.D. dissertation, The Faculty of Theology, Katholieke Universiteit Leuven, 1988).

Christian theology, i.e., one that addresses the most fundamental mystery of Triune self-communication.

In the Barthian tradition, emphasis is given to the inability of finite, human language to meaningfully grasp revelation. Any analogy of being, or real analogy of understanding, is rejected as dangerous to the pure analogy of faith. And this limitation on pure theological language applies to the entire domain of faith, including, of course, the Trinity. For Barth, the "theological" approach to God typified by Feuerbach, which sought to "grasp" revelation, was merely a philosophy exalting the human self as positing God's existence.[28] In Barth's eyes, Feuerbachian "theology" was in fact an anti-theology; and the work of Strauss merely gave the impression that its "theological" author was a "heretic and an unbeliever ... a Central European rejoicing in his learning."[29] Strauss ultimately thought that faith has its reality only in the immanence of human consciousness, and viewed Jesus of Nazareth in a manner of strikingly reduced stature, more "groomed," domesticated, and practicable than the "myths" of the New Testament might suggest.[30] Along with disposing of miraculous elements in the New Testament such as virgin birth and resurrection, Strauss would effectively dispose of the Trinitarian tradition of faith by describing it simply as a misunderstanding.[31] And yet, for Barth, when one is confronted with the objections of a Strauss or a Feuerbach, one is not required to enter into reasoned discourse: "Die rechte Theologie beginnt genau dort, wo die von Strauss und von Feuerbach aufgedeckten Nöte gesehen und dann zum Gelächter geworden sind. So 'liebt' man nämlich solche Männer und ihre Fragen!"[32] It is certainly of merit to be aware of the limitations of human language, but a "Barthian" polemic can reveal a misunderstanding of the negative and limiting aspect of analogical discourse, and render the Trinitarian mystery so unintelligible as to be, in some ways, correspondingly unimportant. If albeit limited theological understanding of a mystery of the faith cannot enter into reasoned discourse with the larger academic community and the broader culture, then this would only seem to diminish the immanent significance of the mystery.

---

[28]   K. Barth, *Die protestantische Theologie im 19. Jahrhundert: Ihre Vorgeschichte und ihre Geschichte* (Zollikon-Zürich: Evangelischer Verlag, 1952); *Protestant Theology in the Nineteenth Century: Its Background and History*, trans. Bowden, with some chapters trans. Cozens and rev. by the editorial staff of SCM Press (London: SCM Press, 1972). For the discussion of Feuerbach see Chapter 14.

[29]   Barth, *Protestant Theology in the Nineteenth Century*, p. 548.

[30]   Ibid., pp. 557-558.

[31]   Ibid.

[32]   Barth, *Die protestantische Theologie im 19. Jahrhundert*, p. 515; trans. Cozens, *Protestant Theology in the Nineteenth Century*, p. 568: "Proper theology begins just at the point where the difficulties disclosed by Strauss and Feuerbach are seen and then laughed at. Thus such men and their questions are 'loved'!"

At a time when many theologians had basically dismissed the Doctrine of the Trinity, and saw no need even to relegate it to the position of an "Appendix" in a theology of God, H. R. Niebuhr issued a surprising challenge: the Doctrine could still be a valuable path for understanding Church History and ecumenical problems.[33] At least Niebuhr saw the value of again raising the question of a Trinitarian theology in order for Christianity to avoid lapsing into various "Unitarianisms."

Recently, Jüngel has restated a rather classical Barthian approach to Trinitarian theology.[34] And Moltmann has also continued a Trinitarian theology very influenced by the Barthian thematic.[35] While Moltmann's earlier work had stronger Barthian themes of non-entrance into reasoned dialogue with and critique of the other arts, sciences, and disciplines in the spectrum of human culture, his later work has been a much more nuanced attempt to bring some more reasoned intelligibility into a view of the church in the Trinitarian history of God's dealings with the world. In a parallel manner, Pannenberg evidences a renewed appreciation for aspects of the traditionally Roman Catholic emphasis on the albeit limited understanding of the Trinitarian mystery.

Hans Küng's "summa" is located in what is often still a fundamentally Barthian problematic tension between the limited intelligibility of doctrines and a commitment to pure faith.[36] He states that his own basic conclusions often coincide with those of Moltmann,[37] who himself is often echoing Barth. Küng's treatment of the Son and the Spirit in the Economic Trinity tends to make them simply interchangeable, rather than offering some measure of intelligible distinction.[38] With Küng's approach, the Trinity is not really a topic of theological speculation.[39]

In perhaps surprising contrast to Küng, D. Brown, a Fellow and Tutor in Theology and Philosophy at Oxford, does not only argue that the Trinity must be a topic of theological speculation, he also argues that classic and orthodox

[33] H. R. Niebuhr, "The Doctrine of the Trinity and the Unity of the Church," *Theology Today* 3 (1946), 371-384.
[34] E. Jüngel, *Gottes Sein ist im Werden. Veranwortliche Rede vom Sein Gottes bei Karl Barth: eine Paraphrase* (Tübingen: Mohr, 1965); *The Doctrine of the Trinity: God's Being in Becoming* (Grand Rapids: Eerdmans, 1976).
[35] J. Moltmann, *Kirche in der Kraft des Geistes: ein Beitrag zur messianischen Ekklesiologie* (Munich: Kaiser, 1975); *The Church in the Power of the Spirit: A Contribution to Messianic Ecclesiology*, trans. Kohl (London: SCM, 1977); *Trinität und Reich Gottes: zur Gotteslehre* (Munich: Kaiser, 1980); *The Trinity and the Kingdom of God*, trans. Kohl (London: SCM, 1981).
[36] H. Küng, *Christ sein* (Munich: Piper, 1974); *On Being a Christian*, trans. Quinn (Garden City: Doubleday, 1976).
[37] Küng, *On Being a Christian*, p. 608, n15.
[38] Ibid., p. 470.
[39] Ibid., p. 476.

Trinitarian doctrine is logically coherent, with sufficient grounds for belief in it as true.[40]

Also in contrast to Küng's approach, in which the Trinity practically ceases to be considered by a speculative theology, the general tendency of "Process Theology" has been to "limit" the Trinity to that which can be speculatively grasped. While Bracken, like Küng, operates as a Catholic theologian, his starting point is not so much influenced by enduring Barthian themes in German theology as it is an almost complete commitment to the reconstruction of theology using Whitehead as the philosophical basis. While many theologians have attempted a synthesis of Whitehead and Christian thought, e.g., Williams, Pittenger, Cobb, Ogden, and Cousins,[41] Bracken has offered what is perhaps the first full-scale, systematic, Trinitarian theology utilizing Whitehead as its philosophical ground.[42] In Bracken's approach, the rational grasp of change in the world is applied to God. This is a fundamental process notion. Accordingly, rather than a "static" Trinity, the three divine persons are such that they are constantly *growing* and thus *changing* in their knowledge and love of one another.[43] Rather than an emphasis on the existence of the Divine Word prior to and independent to the created order, Bracken asserts that the created order is "part of the total reality of the Son" and that the Son "is part of creation."[44] The distinction between the Son as incarnate in Jesus of Nazareth and his presence in each believer is not so much a qualitative one, but a matter of "degree."[45] As Hill has noted, Bracken's commitment to Whiteheadean philosophy has ultimately caused him to posit a sort of physical, and changing, "nature" in every "actual entity," and there is a sense in which such theology projects the changes of human consciousness onto all reality, with the somewhat rationalistic result of a very limited and anthropomorphicized God. With Whitehead's notions of the Primordial and Consequent Natures of God, the result is that God is not God, and the Trinity is not the Trinity, without the world through and in which God actualizes himself in his Consequent Nature; and thus the result is a type of Panentheism. One would certainly not want to give the false impression of a reactionary rejection of the possibility of a creative,

---

[40]   D. Brown, *The Divine Trinity* (La Salla, Ill.: Open Court, 1985).
[41]   D. Williams, *The Spirit and Forms of Love* (New York: Harper and Row, 1968); N. Pittenger, *Process Thought and Christian Faith* (Welwyn, Herts: Nisbet, 1968); J. Cobb, *A Christian Natural Theology Based on the Thought of Alfred North Whitehead* (London: Lutterworth Press, 1966); S. Ogden, *The Reality of God and Other Essays* (New York: Harper and Row, 1963); E. Cousins, ed., *Process Theology: Basic Writings* (New York: Newman Press, 1971).
[42]   J. Bracken, *The Triune God: Persons, Process, and Community* (Lanham, MD: University Press of America, 1985). See also the review of this by W. Hill, in *The Thomist* 51 (1987), 172-176. Hill's critical comments will be echoed here.
[43]   Bracken, *The Triune God*, p. 7.
[44]   Ibid.
[45]   Ibid., p. 53.

insightful, and profound reconstruction of theology along process lines, as if the philosophical bases utilized by Augustine, Aquinas, and the various conciliar formulations were the only ones appropriate for theological reflection. At the same time, the process synthesises of Bracken, and others, far too frequently appear not to have penetrated the meanings of classical formulations, and thus appear unable to undertake a genuine deconstruction and reconstruction of more classical theology.

Also operating within Catholic circles - but in ways quite distinct from Küng and Bracken - Lonergan, Rahner, Fransen, Congar, Hill, and Nicolas have been engaged with fresh explorations of classical Trinitarian doctrine.[46] But Lonergan's Trinitarian theology has remained largely unfinished, while Rahner's programatic creativity has, in part, remained problematic, and both have been criticized for departing too radically from the method and content of the Trinitarian theology of Aquinas. Fransen, Congar, and Hill all certainly operate from within the general methodological principles of thomistic thought, in admirable integration with 20th-century themes, but none of these three, tremendously significant, theologians has attempted a detailed analysis of the interactive relationships of Aquinas' theological methodology and Trinitarian theology. The massive, 1200-page, Trinitarian project of Nicolas is also principally thomistic in orientation, but it is also a very general treatment using the Trinitarian thematic as an integrative one for systematic

---

[46]   B. Lonergan, *Divinarum personarum conceptio analogica* (Rome: Gregorian University Press, 1957) and his *De Deo Trino*. Also of particular importance is K. Rahner, "Zur scholastischen Begrifflichkeit der ungeschaffenen Gnade," *Schriften zur Theologie*, vol. 1 (Einsiedeln, Zürich, Köln: Benzinger Verlag, 1954), pp. 347-375, originally published in *Zeitschrift für katholische Theologie* 63 (1939); "Some Implications of the Scholastic Concept of Uncreated Grace," *Theological Investigations*, vol. 1, trans. Ernst (Baltimore: Helicon Press, 1961) pp. 319-346; "Bemerkungen zum dogmatischen Traktat 'De Trinitate,'" *Schriften zur Theologie*, vol. 4 (Einsiedeln, Zürich, Köln: Benzinger Verlag, 1960), pp. 103-133; "Remarks on the Dogmatic Treatise 'De Trinitate,'" *Theological Investigations*, vol. 4, trans. Smyth (Baltimore: Helicon Press; London: Darton, Longman and Todd, 1966), pp. 77-102; "Der dreifaltige Gott als transzendenter Urgrund der Heilsgeschichte," Kapitel 5 in *Mysterium Salutis: Grundriss heilsgeschichtlicher Dogmatik*, vol. 2, ed. Feiner and Löhrer (Einsiedeln, Zürich, Köln: Benzinger Verlag, 1967), pp. 317-401; *The Trinity*, trans. Donceel (New York: Herder and Herder, 1970); P. Fransen, *The New Life of Grace*, trans. DuPont, Foreword by J. MacQuarrie (London: Geoffrey Chapman, 1969); Y. Congar, *Je crois en l'Esprit Saint*, 3 vols. (Paris: Cerf, 1980); W. Hill, *Proper Relations to the Indwelling Divine Persons* (Washington, D.C.: The Thomist Press, 1955); *The Three-Personed God: The Trinity as a Mystery of Salvation* (Washington, D.C.: The Catholic University of America Press, 1982); J. Nicolas, *Synthèse dogmatique: de la Trinité à la Trinité* (Paris: Beauchesne, 1985). See also D. Merriell, *To the Image of the Trinity: A Study in the Development of Aquinas' Teaching*. Studies and Texts, 96 (Toronto: Pontifical Institute of Mediaeval Studies, 1990) and O. Gonzales de Cardedal, *Teologia y Antropologia, el hombre 'imagen de Dios' en el pensamiento de Santo Tomás*, Estudios de teologia 1 (Madrid: Editorial Moneda y Credito, 1967). In addition, although it is a brief work, J. Daniélou, *La Trinité et le mystere de l'existence* (Bruges: Desclée de Brouwer, 1968); *God's Life in Us*, trans. Leggat (Denville, N.J.: Dimension Books, 1969) presents an exceptionally rich and profound Trinitarian meditation. There is also the recent, masterful contribution in the domain of orthodox theology by B. Bobrinskoy, *Le mystère de la Trinité: cours de théologie orthodoxe* (Paris: Cerf, 1986).

theology, and, furthermore, in its specific sections addressing theological method and the Trinity there is a problematic tension in Nicolas, even as in Aquinas, regarding the tendency to objectivize metaphysical analogies in Trinitarian theology.

It may well be, additionally, that a major need of theological ecumenism at present is for a reappropriation of the theological method and content of Aquinas, and this may particularly be the case with regard to the fundamental Christian doctrine of the Trinity. The stereotypic Protestant critique of Aquinas' Trinitarian theology is that it embodies a rationalistic view of faith and an objectification of metaphysical analogies. Vos has recently argued very well that the Protestant stereotype of Aquinas as advocating a rationalistic view of faith is simply incorrect,[47] and one could well extend this criticism to say that even within Roman Catholicism the Neoscholastic stereotype of Aquinas as advocating an Aristotelian "science" of theology is simply incorrect. It is the case that the theological method and the Trinitarian theology of Aquinas stand as a heritage to both Roman Catholicism and the Reformed churches, from a period pre-dating the major divisions in Western Christendom. It may well be that both Protestant and Roman Catholic theologians would find much more in common, after a careful analysis of Aquinas' theological method and Trinitarian theology, than would generally be expected.

Thus the need for a revitalized theology of the Trinity continues.

Since the Trinitarian theology of Aquinas has seldom been grasped in an accurate manner, despite centuries of commentary, it is appropriate that contemporary theology at least strive for this goal before undertaking a revisionist, deconstructionist, or reconstructionist program.

The value of Aquinas' Trinitarian theology lies both in the albeit limited content it is able to achieve and, perhaps more importantly, in what is revealed about Christian consciousness and the structure of faithed-intentionality as one embarks upon the arduous path of seeking some understanding of ultimate Mystery. The theme here is an important one often overlooked even by late-20th-century thomistic scholars: even as, for Aquinas, the natural structure of the agent intellect cannot be known by the human subject directly, in- and of-itself, but only indirectly, as it is only able to reflect upon itself by means of reflecting upon its operations in coming-to-know - and thus the end point of metaphysics is also the end point of philosophical anthropology; so too the theologically considered structure of the human subject as "imago Dei" with a "supernaturally augmented" agent intellect, because of the "light" of divine grace and revelation, cannot be known in- and of-itself, directly, but only indirectly, as this structure is able,

---

[47]   A. Vos, *Aquinas, Calvin and Contemporary Protestant Thought: A Critique of Protestant Views on the Thought of Thomas Aquinas* (Grand Rapids: Eerdmans, 1985).

somehow, to reflect on its operations in "coming-to-know" the Trinitarian Mystery, and thus the end-point of Trinitarian theology is also the end-point of theological anthropology. Since Christian understanding of the Trinity is so radically a matter of faith, a reflection on what is involved in this Trinitarian-directed assent of faith may well help to ease stereotypic misunderstandings of basic Christian intentionality. It may well be that there is a more profound negativity of *agnosia* and a more profound dialectical movement of remotion in Aquinas' understanding of faith, theology, and the Trinity than even that presented by Barth. The negation in Aquinas may be even more profound than in Barth precisely because Aquinas first affirms the entire domain of natural, rational knowledge and the necessity of entrance into reasoned discourse. Then he negates the adequacy of this domain, even when enlightened by faith, for an adequate understanding of God; but also recovers this domain as all the human subject can adequately undertake and thus must undertake, even though it ultimately faces negation. It may well be that this spiraling dialectic in Aquinas is far more profound than the dialectics of Barth and offers far greater insight into the structure of human consciousness and language than is possible with Barth. More than in any other of his works, Aquinas presents this spiraling dialectic in his *Expositio* of the *De Trinitate* of Boethius. In order to understand this *Expositio*, some entrance into the classical world of Boethius' *De Trinitate* will be required.

CHAPTER TWO

BOETHIUS: THE THEOLOGICAL TRACTATES

Anicius Manlius Torquatus Severinus Boethius (ca. 480-524) was the son of a former Roman consul, and Boethius himself eventually served as consul under Theoderic the Ostrogoth. It was the 15th-century humanist Lorenzo Valla who coined the now-famous description of Boethius as the "last of the Romans, first of the scholastics,"[1] in tribute to Boethius' project of transmitting in Latin the complete works of Plato and Aristotle, along with a synthesis of their positions. Before Boethius, the Latin West had practically none of the works of either Plato or Aristotle available in translation. And Boethius attempted more than mere translation; he undertook a vast project of commentary. Although his Roman contemporaries were singularly uninterested in these projects, Boethius' commentaries on Aristotle's *Categories* and *On Interpretation* proved to be the basis of much of the West's knowledge of Aristotelian logic for the next six centuries.

On September 1, 522, Boethius received the important administrative post of Master of the Offices, under the Emperor Theoderic, a position created under Diocletian. In this post, Boethius held extensive powers in relation to members of the Senate, controlling access to the Emperor, and regulating the appointments of provincial governors. In this position Boethius was able to protect the wealth of his friends in the Senate from the greedy desires of many of the palace courtiers. Shortly after attaining the post of Master of the Offices, a certain Cyprian, a private secretary of Theoderic, denounced Albinus, a member of the Senate and friend of Boethius, for having corresponded with persons close to the Eastern Emperor, Justin (Justinian I), in a manner amounting to treason and conspiracy. Albinus denied the charge, but was declared guilty by Theoderic without a proper legal procedure. Boethius then boldly spoke in defence of Albinus, saying that if Albinus was indeed guilty of such a crime, so was he, and even the entire Senate. Cyprian then declared that Boethius had known of the correspondence of Albinus, but

---

[1] Cited by H. Chadwick, *Boethius: The Consolations of Music, Logic, Theology, and Philosophy* (Oxford: Clarendon Press, 1981), p. xi. This work is a very valuable source as a rare combination of historical, philosophical, and theological erudition. See also the excellent collection of studies in M. Gibson, ed., *Boethius: His Life, Thought and Influence* (Oxford: Basil Blackwell, 1981).

suppressed the evidence and did not report it to Theoderic. Given the already strained relationship between Theoderic and the Senate, the Emperor took advantage of the situation as an excuse to liquidate the entire Senate. Added to the charge of conspiracy against Boethius, was one of delving into "black magic" in order to further his own designs. Boethius responded that such a charge was unfounded and contemptible, but it is easy to see how such a charge could have arisen. First of all, accusations of treason and sorcery were commonly linked in this period, and, secondly, the writings of Boethius on fate and providence had discussed the powers of divine spirits, and his *Commentary* on Aristotle's *On Interpretation* had recognized that the stars exercised a determining power not only over animal life, but over human life as well, particularly in the constriction of free will. Since in 519 a massive comet, visible in Rome, had passed through the heavens, and since such celestial events were generally interpreted in antiquity as foretelling a change of dynasty or some other disaster,[2] and since the anxiety-filled Theoderic most likely regarded the comet as a portent of doom for his dynasty, the accusation against Boethius of practicing "black arts" would have been a particularly dangerous one.

Cyprian, the accusor of Albinus and Boethius, was eventually appointed Treasurer of the Royal Household, and then Master of the Offices, the post previously held by Boethius, as Cyprian seemed to Theoderic to be a model of loyal service.

Albinus and Boethius were arrested, with Boethius being placed in prison in Pavia. Boethius was never called to defend himself, and the Senate Court assembled by Theoderic in Rome passed the death sentence, an act that was regarded by Boethius as pathetically timid, as it had been he who had sought to protect the interests of the noble members of the Senate. After a long period in prison, he was tortured and put to a brutal death. A note in the Ravenna chronicle of the *Anonymus Valesianus* records that while in prison, most likely in Pavia, a cord was twisted around the head of Boethius so that his eyeballs burst from their sockets, and blows from a club finished the execution.[3] According to the first edition of the *Liber Pontificalis*, Theoderic ordered that the body of Boethius be hidden.[4] If this is so, it may be because Theoderic was aware that, as an Arian king, his execution of Boethius, whose own *Opuscula Sacra* were already well known, and who was prominently

---

[2]   Cf. Origen, *Contra Celsum* I, 59, and discussion in Chadwick, *Boethius*, p. 50.

[3]   Chadwick, *Boethius*, p. 55. Chadwick also refers to the *Secret History* [*Anecdota* xvi, 26] of Procopius, which states that under Theodora's orders a prisoner had been tortured by having leather twisted around his temples "until he felt as if his eyeballs had jumped out." Chadwick concludes that, "this is evidently the method applied to the wretched Boethius" (p. 55), although to literally apply such pressure until the eyeballs pop out would itself require a level of pressure that would crush the skull, and so that particular extent of the report in the *Anonymus Valesianus* is probably an exaggeration.

[4]   See Chadwick, *Boethius*, p. 56.

associated with the Roman Catholic Church, could be seen as an instance of martyrdom.[5]

By the 9th century, Ado of Vienne records that Boethius died "for Catholic piety."[6] In the 10th century, the tower in Pavia where he had been imprisoned came to be venerated as a sacred place of martyrdom. Also in the 10th century, he had come to be so revered as a "saint" and scholar of the Latin West, that his bones were removed to the Church of S. Pietro in Ciel d'Oro (St. Peter in Caelo Aureo), the same church that had acquired the relics of St. Augustine during the 8th century. In the 14th century, an anonymous chronicler of Pavia wrote that after his decapitation, Boethius had carried his own head into the church of S. Pietro in Ciel d'Oro. In the late medieval calendar of Pavia, the feast of a "St. Severinus" is commemorated on October 23rd, but this date is also that for a St. Severinus of Cologne, according to the Roman Martyrology, and thus it is hard to say if the calendar of Pavia was meant to refer to Boethius.[7]

Aside from his *De Consolatione Philosophiae*, one of the greatest masterpieces in western literature, let alone of "pre-execution prison literature," Boethius also wrote five theological tractates of enormous importance.[8] It is particularly in these tractates that Boethius reveals himself as the "first of the scholastics," integrating Aristotelian logic, but also - and perhaps mainly - forging a type of Christian Neoplatonism, greatly in debt to Proclus, though not simply repeating Proclus. The exact titles of these tractates present some problems, as does the question of their original numbering and order. The problem of titles and order arises because many of the manuscripts contain no titles, and they are not numbered as if to indicate a certain order. And the often published numbering of the tractates does not reflect their chronological order. The Migne edition is particularly confusing with regard to the titles of these tractates and their ordering. The "Table of Contents" in the Migne Edition lists the following titles in the following order: 1) *De duabus naturis et una persona*, 2) *De unitate Dei*, 3) *An Pater*,

---

    [5]   Cf. J. Zeiller, "Les églises ariennes de Rome à l'époque de la domination gothique," *Mélanges de l'école française de Rome* 24 (1905), 127-146. See also W. Bark, "Theoderic vs. Boethius: Vindication and Apology," *American Historical Review* 49 (1944), 410-426.
    [6]   Ado of Vienne, PL 123, c. 107C, cited by Chadwick, *Boethius*, p. 54.
    [7]   Chadwick, *Boethius*, p. 54; W. Bark, "The Legend of Boethius' Martyrdom," *Speculum* 21 (1946), 312-317; H. Patch, "The Beginnings of the Legend of Boethius," *Speculum* 22 (1947), 443-445.
    [8]   Editions can be found in Boethius, *Opera*. Corpus Christianorum, Series Latina, vol. 94, ed. L. Bieler (Turnholt: Brepols, 1957); *Opera Omnia*, PL 64; *Theological Tractates*, ed. and trans. H. Stewart, E. Rand, and S. Tester, Loeb Classical Library, Latin, vol. 74 (Cambridge, MA: Harvard University Press, 1973). Migne's PL 64 is not regarded as a good edition. The 1918 English translation of Rand's edition has been revised by S. Tester in the 1973 Loeb Edition. See also the review by J. O'Donnell, in *American Journal of Philology* 98 (1977), 77-79. All references will be to the 1973 Loeb edition. See also *Die theologischen Traktaten*, ed. and trans. M. Elsasser (Hamburg: Meiner, 1988).

Filius, Spiritus sanctus, de Deo affimari possint? 4) *An bonum sit omne quod est, sive De Hebdomadibus*, and 5) *Brevis complexio fidei.* But the titles and their order given in the text of Migne are: 1) *Quomodo Trinitas unus Deus ac non tres Dii*, 2) *Utrum Pater et Filius et Spiritus Sanctus de divinitatae substantialiter praedicentur liber, ad S. Joannem diaconum ecclesiae romanae*, 3) *Quomodo substantiae in eo quod sint, bonae sint*, 4) *Brevis fidei christianae complexio*, and 5) *Liber de persona et duabus naturis, contra Eutychen et Nestorium, ad Joannem diaconum ecclesiae romanae.* The order in which the tractates actually appear in the Migne edition, but not the order in the Migne "Table of Contents," is the same order as in the Loeb Classical Library edition. But the titles of the tractates in the text of Migne are slightly different from the titles in the Loeb edition, and this can generate some confusion.[9] The confusion can make it more difficult to sort through references in the secondary literature. The point of numbers, titles, and actual sequence in which the tractates were written is also of importance in order to see the relationships of the tractates, sense more unified themes, and appreciate that Tractate I, *De Trinitate*, is probably the *last* of the tractates to be written. It may be that Aquinas' unfinished commentaries on the two tractates, which came to be known simply as *De Hebdomadibus* and *De Trinitate* were also part of a larger, more integrated project of Aquinas seeking to merge participationist metaphysics and Trinitarian theology, along with sophisticated reflections on theological method.

Exactly what numbering, if any, and what titles, if any, Boethius actually gave these tractates is unknown. But for present purposes, the actual order and numbering of both the Migne and Loeb editions will be used, while the titles used will be those of the later Loeb edition. It should be noted that the title of Tractate I is thus not technically *De Trinitate*, but this is the title by which the work was known in most of medieval usage. Also, the most correct title of Tractate III is not *De Hebdomadibus*, but it came to be referred to in this manner. Finally, it should be noted that Tractate V, *Contra Eutychen et Nestorium*, is also at times referred to in the secondary literature by the title, *De duabus naturis in una persona christi*, or *Liber de persona et duabus naturis*, and also by reference to its opening words: "Anxie te quidem diuque sustinui."

---

[9]   In the Loeb edition by Rand, the titles and the order of the tractates are as follows: 1) *Trinitas unus Deus ac non tres Dii (The Trinity is One God not Three Gods)*, and this is the *De Trinitate*, 2) *Utrum Pater et Filius et Spiritus sanctus de divinitate substantialiter praedicentur (Whether Father, Son, and Holy Spirit are Substantially Predicated of the Divinity)*, 3) *Quomodo substantiae in eo quod sint bonae sint cum non sint substantialia bona (How Substances are Good in Virtue of their Existence Without Being Substantial Goods)*, also known as the *De Hebdomadibus*, 4) *De fide catholica (On the Catholic Faith)*, and 5) *Contra Eutychen et Nestorium domino sancto ac venerabili patri Iohanni diacono Boethius filius (Against Eutyches and Nestorius, to His Saintly Master and Reverend Father, John the Deacon, From His Son Boethius)*.

In reference to the works of Boethius, Cassiodorus remarked, "scripsit librum de sancta trinitate et capita quaedam dogmatica et librum contra Nestorium" ("He wrote a book on the Sacred Trinity, and some dogmatic chapters, and a book against Nestorius").[10] If the theological works of Boethius are to be so divided, one may well ask what the structure of his original "book on the Trinity" was. The evidence is that what came to be known as Tractate I, *De Trinitate* and Tractate II, on logical predication in Trinitarian theology, and Tractate III, *De Hebdomadibus* were originally part of a unified intention on the part of Boethius, and at least came to be regarded as Trinitarian tractates in a sort of unified "book." The reference in Cassiodorus to "a book against Nestorius" is clearly to the *Contra Eutychen et Nestorium* (also known as the *De duabus naturis in una persona*), and the reference to "some dogmatic chapters" would seem to be to *De Fide Catholica*.[11]

The Chronology, Motivation, and Contents of the Theological Tractates

The chronology of the tractates is debated. Tractate I, *De Trinitate*, is probably the last to be written, with Tractate II, *Ultrum Pater et Filius et Spiritus Sanctus*, immediately preceding it. Tractate IV, *De Fide Catholica*, is probably the first to be written, as it is not a systematic reflection. Tractate III, *De Hebdomadibus*, and Tractate V, *Contra Eutychaen et Nestorium*, most likely preceded Tractates I and II. Although it is difficult to say whether Tractate III preceded or followed Tractate V, a reasonable chronology of the tractates is: IV, V, III, II, I.[12] Thus the reflections of Boethius begin with

---

[10] Cassiodorus, in a fragment called the *Anecdoton Holderi*, which was discovered by Alfred Holder and edited by H. Usener, *Anecdoton Holderi, ein Beitrag zur Geschichte Roms in ostgothischer Zeit. Festschrift zur Begrüssung der 32. Versammlung deutscher Philologen und Schulmänner zu Wiesbaden* (Bonn, 1877). The text of the *Anecdoton* is also available in *Cassiodori . . . Opera I*, Corpus Christianorum, vol. 96, ed. A. Fridh and J. Halporn (Turnhout: Brepols, 1973), pp. v-vi. See also discussion in Chadwick, *Boethius*, p. 175; and J. O'Donnell, *Cassiodorus* (Los Angeles: University of California Press, 1978), pp. 259-266.

[11] Cf. W. Bark, "Boethius' Fourth Tractate, The So-Called 'De fide catholica,'" *Harvard Theological Review* 39 (1946), 55-69; H. Chadwick, "The Authenticity of Boethius' Fourth Tractate 'De fide catholica,'" *Journal of Theological Studies* 31 (1980), 551-556.

[12] Cf. Chadwick, *Boethius*, pp. 211, 180. On the dating and sequence of the tractates, see A. McKinlay, "Stylistic Tests and the Chronology of the Works of Boethius," *Harvard Studies in Classical Philology* 18 (1907), 123-156. On the historical circumstances of the tractates, see V. Schurr, *De Trinitätslehre des Boethius im Lichte der 'skythischen Kontroversen,'* Forschungen z. Christlichen Literatur u. Dogmengeschichte XVIII (Paderborn, 1933), pp. 76, 105-227. See also A. Kappelmacher, "Der schriftstellerische Plan des Boethius," *Wiener Studien* 46 (1929), 215-225; I. Crämer-Rugenberg, *Die Substanzmetaphysik des Boethius in den Opuscula sacra* (Ph.D. dissertation, University of Cologne, 1967). It should also be noted that all "five" of the tractates are now regarded as authentic writings of Boethius. See J. Mair, "The Text of the *Opuscula Sacra*," in *Boethius: His Life, Thought and Influence*, p. 206. See also L. Obertello, *Severino Boezio*, 2 vols. (Genoa: Academia Ligura di Scienze e Lettere, 1974). For a different

kerygma and dogma (the authorities) and develop into systematics (by means of reason). In any case the exact sequence of the Tractates is not as important as the point that they represent an integrated attempt at philosophical and systematic Trinitarian theology.

Tractate IV: De Fide Catholica

Tractate IV, *De Fide Catholica*, is mainly a work which echoes Augustine, over and over, in a summary of what is to be believed. The central point of Catholic faith, as here proposed, is the Trinity, as existing before creation and before time, as One God. Boethius then considers creation, the fall of the angels, the fall of Adam, and a summary of the Old Testament, Incarnation, and redemption. The style of this Tractate is not systematic, philosophical theology, but much more one of kerygma, evangelical pronouncement, and confession. It is probably the earliest of the tractates, and intended not for publication as much as a brief statement of the catechetical instruction Boethius had received from John the Deacon, and its date would seem to be ca. 512. It is not an apologetic theology as much as it is mystagogia. There is no attempt to bring reason and faith into an overarching harmony.

Tractate V: Contra Eutychen et Nestorium

The motivation behind Boethius' *De Trinitate* seems to have been the Trinitarian dispute of 519 concerning the formula "unus ex Trinitate carne passus," which certain monks from Scythia regarded as orthodox; and the tractate *De Trinitate*, as the last of the tractates to be written, is generally thought to have been finished before 522.

From 512 to about 515, the commander of the Gothic army was Vitalian, whose power was checked in 515, but who returned again to a position of military domination in 518, the same year Justin became the Eastern Emperor.[13] Vitalian came from the Danube delta in the Dobrudja, and among his associates there was a group of "Scythian" monks, i.e., they were Goths from the Dobrudja. One of this group was Dionysius Exiguus, who introduced the "Anno Domini" calender. In Constantinople, the theological leader of this group of monks was Maxentius, who was convinced that his Trinitarian theology, largely based on Augustine, could resolve the dispute

---

view of the ordering of the tractates see L. Obertello, *Boezio: la Consolazione della Filosofia, e gli Opuscoli Teologici* (Milan: Rusconi, 1979), who gives the order of the tractates as V, II, I, III, IV.

[13]   Chadwick, *Boethius*, p. 186.

between the East and West. The "Scythian" monks who had originally been in the company of Vitalian, went with Maxentius to Constantinople in about 519 to seek the help of Justin in their cause, who then sent them to Pope Hormisdas to get a sense of the possibilities of reconciliation. The group was not well received in Rome, and Hormisdas was advised not to add anything to the Chalcedonian formula. However, after the time of Hormisdas, the more influential theologians among the Roman clergy came to regard the theopaschite formula of the "Scythian" monks - "Christ is one of the Trinity who suffered in the flesh" - much more positively, and this is most likely due in no small part to Boethius' Tractate V, *Contra Eutychen et Nestorium*, which was most likely written sometime in the period 518-521.

Tractate V is dedicated to a "John the Deacon" of Rome, who, at the time the work was written, was a dear friend and the spiritual father of Boethius.[14] This "John" was one of the seven deacons of the city of Rome, and he enjoyed a reputation as a man of serious scholarship. It is most likely that he is identical with Pope Hormisdas' successor, Pope John I (523-526).[15] It is also likely that at the time of this John's election to the Roman papacy, Boethius, while still in good graces with Theoderic and still occupying his high governmental position in Ravenna, would have helped the election to receive the official approbation of Theoderic. The *Opuscula Sacra* of Boethius survived because they were collected by John the Deacon in Rome, and the five tractates were probably made available by him in Rome as early as 523.[16] It was on August 6, 523 that Pope Hormisdas died, and his successor, John I, was a member of the pro-Byzantine circle of Roman clergy which, along with Boethius, wished to see some resolution of the political and theological - mainly Trinitarian - conflicts between East and West. The politico-religious complexities of the situation were compounded by the fact that Theoderic was an Arian emperor in the West, while Justin was seeking to eliminate Arianism in the East, a policy which was naturally disliked by Theoderic. Pope John I and Boethius were committed to an orthodox Trinitarian formulation which was equated by Theoderic with a type of treason against Rome. During one high point of the conflict between Theoderic and Justin, Pope John I, five other bishops, and four of the most senior senators were sent by Theoderic to Constantinople to inform Justin that unless all harassment of Arians in the East ceased, Theoderic would destroy the Byzantine churches in Italy. The tone of the message seemed to imply the possible murder of the Byzantine Catholics in Italy as well.[17] Pope John undertook this journey in the deepest anguish imaginable. When he met the

---

[14]   Ibid., p. 26.
[15]   Ibid., p. 28.
[16]   Ibid., p. 255.
[17]   Ibid., p. 59.

Eastern Emperor, Justin bowed in a deep prostration and they exchanged a kiss of greeting. It was the first visit of a bishop of Rome to Constantinople. John was seated at the right hand of the Emperor in the Cathedral, and celebrated Mass in Latin there on Easter Day. Additionally, John placed the crown on Justin's head; an act that Theoderic certainly heard of immediately, and would have reacted to as an act of treason. Justin actually agreed to most of the proposals of Pope John in order to restore peace; except the one particular demand of Theoderic that the Arians in the East who had been pressured into joining the Byzantine Church be permitted to return to their Arian communities.

When Pope John I then returned to Ravenna, Theoderic declared that he should be *in offensa sua* - a technical term for the withdrawal of the king's favor in cases of disloyalty. Theoderic then ordered that all of the other bishops and senators who had accompanied Pope John I be thrown into prison and tortured. While Pope John I may have escaped the tortures of which Theoderic was capable, he nonetheless died in Theoderic's dungeon in Ravenna. The response of the Roman Catholic faithful was to immediately regard John I as a martyr. As his funeral procession passed through the city, even senators tore pieces of his vestments as relics, and there were reports of miraculous power emanating from his funeral bier. Such events were extremely disturbing to the already distraught Theoderic who, only about one hundred days after John's death, on August 30, 526, ordered that Arians should take possession of all the Roman Catholic churches in Ravenna; but on that very day Theoderic died.[18]

The Boethian Tractate V, *Contra Eutychen et Nestorium, Domino Sancto ac Venerabili Patri Iohanni Diacono Boethius Filius (A Treatise Against Eutyches and Nestorius, To His Saintly Master and Reverend Father John the Deacon From His Son Boethius)*, begins by explaining its origin at a meeting which both Boethius and John attended: "Anxie te quidem diuque sustinui, ut de ea quae in conventu mota est quaestione loqueremur" ("I have been long and anxiously waiting for you that we might discuss the problem which was raised at the meeting").[19] Boethius then refers to a letter which was read at that meeting, and this letter was most likely the one addressed to Pope Symmachus from a Byzantine bishop in 512 (or 513), which expressed a

---

[18] Gregory the Great records a story in his *Dialogues* IV, 31, about a hermit who at the very hour of Theoderic's death saw a vision of the king, stripped of his insignia and shoes, with his hands bound, being taken by Pope John, and dropped into the "Vulcani olla" ("cauldron of Vulcan") - evidently a nearby volcano regarded as one of the chimneys of hell. This is cited by Chadwick, *Boethius*, pp. 62-63.

[19] Boethius, Tractate V, *Contra Eutychen et Nestorium* (p. 72). All references to the theological tractates of Boethius are to the Loeb Classical Library Edition (1973), with page numbers given in parentheses.

dogmatic course between the heresies of Eutyches and Nestorius.[20] The Tractate V of Boethius may have been written in the same year, 512-513, or some six years later. In this letter, the Eastern bishop, probably a Metropolitan, proposed an understanding of Christ as both *of* and *in* two natures. At the meeting in 512 when the letter was received and discussed, in some storm and turmoil, Boethius was shocked that the real problems involved were not being analyzed at all. During the meeting, Boethius, as he states in this Tractate, could not see the face of Pope Symmachus, and was not sure how he should publically react, and so, he says, "I held my peace, fearing lest I should be rightly set down as insane if I held out for being sane among those madmen."[21] Appalled at the ignorance of those at the meeting who were supposed to be able to discuss technical terms in Trinitarian theology, Boethius set himself to writing Tractate V and submitting it to John the Deacon for his consideration. By the end of the 6th century, Gregory the Great was proclaiming the formula that Christ was both *of* and *in* two natures,[22] no doubt in no small measure because of the influence of Boethius' fifth tractate.

In Tractate V, Boethius first clarifies the meaning of the term "nature," then explores the meaning of "substance" and "person." For Boethius, both Nestorius and Eutyches treated "nature" and "person" as the same thing, and this is the basis of each of their errors.

For Boethius, "nature" may be predicated of physical bodies, or substances, whether corporeal or not, or of everything that exists in any way. Since "nature" thus has three manners of predication, it is important to clarify the way in which it is used in Trinitarian theology. When it is used to refer to all things that exist, this includes both substances and accidents, and since there are no accidents in God, this sense of the term cannot be used in Trinitarian theology. "Nature" as predicated of corporeal substances also is not completely appropriate for Trinitarian theology.

A "person" cannot exist apart from "nature," and since a "person" cannot exist in "accidents" alone, "person" can only be predicated of "substance." But again, some substances are corporeal and others incorporeal; and of incorporeal substances only one is immutable by nature, i.e., God. "Person" cannot be predicated of an inanimate substance, nor merely of any living thing, nor of animals alone, but only of rational substances, which include human beings, angels, and God. Also, "person" cannot be predicated of universals, but only of particulars. Thus a person is "naturae rationabilis

---

[20] The letter is preserved in an awkward 6th-century Latin translation printed in T. Herold, ed., *Orthodoxographia* (Basel, 1555), pp. 906-909. The letter is undated and could be from 512 or 513. It makes a plea for a constructive and positive Roman policy, and for a clarification of theological terminology. See discussion in Chadwick, *Boethius*, pp. 181-183.

[21] Boethius, Tractate V, *Contra Eutychen et Nestorium* (p. 72).

[22] Gregory the Great, *Homilies on the Gospels*, 38, 3.

individua substantia" ("an individual substance of a rational nature.")[23] Thus the Latin "persona" means, for Boethius, what the Greek "hypostasis" means.

A thing has "subsistence" when it does not require accidents in order to exist. Genera and species as such only have subsistence, while actually existing individual substances, such as a human being, have subsistence and accidents. Thus a human being has essence, subsistence, substance, person, and accidents. And God is an essence, for it is from God that the being of all other things proceeds; a subsistence, for he subsists in absolute independence; and a single substance, with no accidents - but there are three hypostases in God, and three persons, and thus there is one essence of the Trinity, three "substances" and three persons.

For Boethius, Nestorius affirmed that in Christ "person" was twofold, for in understanding a twofold nature he considered a twofold person. For Boethius, however, the one person of Christ has two natures. Eutyches held, on the other hand, that Christ could not have two natures, but only a divine nature, and that therefore the person of Christ was only divine. Some Eutychians held that Christ consisted *of* two natures but not *in* two natures, so that there was never a mixture or confusion of the two. For Boethius, "Catholici vero utrumque rationabiliter confitentur, nam et ex utrisque naturis Christum et in utrisque consistere" ("But Catholics in accordance with reason confess both, for they say that Christ consists both of and in two natures").[24]

Boethius is perfectly orthodox in his formulation, and yet his desire to bring reason to bear on Trinitarian theology at times goes so far as to seem to "prove" dogmatic formulations. He argues that there are only four possibilities for Christ: two natures and two persons, as Nestorius says; or one person and one nature, as Eutyches says; or two natures but one person, as the Catholic faith believes; or one nature and two persons, which is impossible. Boethius states that he has "refuted" Nestorius and shown the position of Eutyches to be "impossible," and thus the position of the Catholic faith must be true, i.e., that there are two natures, and thus two substances, but one person.[25] But, of course, this cannot be proven.

Tractate III: De Hebdomadibus

Tractate III, *Quomodo Substantiae in Eo Quod Sint Bona Cum Non Sint Substantialia Bona,* also known as *De Hebdomadibus,* is very brief but perhaps the most technical of the five tractates. This work also seems to be addressed to John the Deacon, apparently to answer a question put to

---

[23] Boethius, Tractate V, *Contra Eutychen et Nestorium* (p. 84).
[24] Ibid. p. 114.
[25] Ibid. pp. 120-121.

Boethius by John concerning another work by Boethius which was called "Hebdomads." In this response to the question raised, Boethius reveals part of his approach to deeply speculative issues:

> Prohinc tu ne sis obscuritatibus brevitatis adversus, quae cum sint arcani fida custodia tum id habent commodi, quod cum his solis qui digni sunt conloquuntur.[26]

The "secret doctrine" which he seems concerned to protect is the notion that everything that exists has moral value as a good, and that all particular goods are good insofar as they participate in the Idea of the Good.

In this work Boethius also makes the distinction between "esse" and "id quod est,"[27] and he holds that "ipsum esse" does not participate in anything. He also distinguishes participation in absolute "esse" from participation in the "something else" which constitutes the particular "id quod est" of the thing. Further, while in the finite order all things that exist participate in goodness, all finite entities need not be "just," for "justice" follows upon action rather than upon existence as such. The technical procedure of this Tractate III was of great influence in itself, for Boethius' approach was to analyze the arguments by making explicit the fundamental presuppositions and definitions upon which they rest.

Tractate II: Utrum Pater et Filius et Spiritus Sanctus

Tractate II is the briefest of the five tractates, and it is less theologically and philosophically technical than Tractate I. It may have been a preparatory exercise for Tractate I, or a particular response to a question raised by John the Deacon.[28] The second tractate is almost entirely a mosaic of phrases from Augustine,[29] but this is merged with a concern for more Aristotelian logic which is not to be found in Augustine.

Boethius begins by asking whether the terms "Father," "Son," and "Holy Spirit" are predicated substantially of the divinity. The question concerns whether the three divine Persons are three "substances," or whether there is only one "substance" in God. Boethius responds that each of the divine

---

[26]   Boethius, Tractate III, *Quomodo Substantiae*, i.e., *De Hebdomadibus* (p. 38). Thus do not take objection to obscurities consequent on brevity, which are the treasure house of secret doctrine and have the advantage that they will only speak to those who are worthy.

[27]   Cf. P. Hadot, "La distinction de l'être et de l'étant dans le 'De Hebdomadibus' de Boèce," in *Miscellanea Mediaevalia*, ed. P. Wilpert (Berlin: Walter De Gruyter, 1963), pp. 147-153.

[28]   Chadwick notes that in some early MSS the first word is not "quaero" ("I ask"), but "quaeris" ("you ask"), *Boethius*, p. 212.

[29]   Augustine, *De Trinitate*, Book 5 and *The City of God*, Book 11, Chapter 24.

Persons is a "substance," but the three together only form one "substance." Thus, everything that is predicated of the divine substance must be common to the three divine Persons. This means that whatever terms are predicated of any one divine Person - such as truth, goodness, justice, immutability, and omnipotence - apply to the entire divine "substance." But Boethius recognizes that some terms are predicated only of one of the divine Persons, for example, the terms "Father," "Son," and "Holy Spirit" are predicated of particular divine Persons, but not of all three. Thus Boethius proposes that "Father," "Son," and "Holy Spirit" are not predicated of God "substantially," but in some other way. Boethius concludes, further, that "Trinity" cannot be substantially predicated of God, because "The Father" is not "Trinity," nor is "The Son," nor is "The Holy Spirit." The names of the particular divine Persons, and even the term "Trinity" itself, are not predicated of God "substantially," but "relatively,"[30] i.e., by means of the "relations" of the divine Persons. The problem is how such "relations" can be considered some*things* of which distinct predications are possible.

Boethius concludes this brief Tractate on Trinitarian predication with a humble appeal to John the Deacon, which also makes explicit reference to the task of finding a harmonious construction of faith and reason:

> Haec si se recte et ex fide habent, ut me instruas peto; aut si aliqua re forte diversus es, diligentius intuere quae dicta sunt et fidem si poterit rationemque coniunge.[31]

One can well imagine how Aquinas would have been impressed with this ending: the statement of the ideal task of Aquinas' theological project.

Tractate I: De Trinitate

Tractate I begins with a merger of metaphors of "divine light" and the "spark of human intelligence" which will be repeated by Aquinas with exceptional frequency:

---

[30] For Boethius, Tractate II, *Utrum Pater et Filius et Spiritus Sanctus* (p. 36): "Quo fit ut neque pater, neque filius neque spiritus sanctus neque trinitas de deo substantialiter praedicetur, sed ut dictum est ad aliquid" ("Thus it follows that neither 'Father' nor 'Son' nor 'Holy Spirit' nor 'Trinity' is predicated of God substantially, but only relatively, as we have said").

[31] Ibid. (p. 36). If these things are right and in accordance with the faith, I pray that you confirm me; or if you are in any point of another opinion, examine carefully what has been said and, if possible, reconcile faith and reason.

Investigatam diutissime quaestionem, quantum nostrae mentis igniculum lux divina dignata est, formatam rationibus litterisque mandatam offerendam vobis communicandamque curavi tam vestri cupidus iudicii quam nostri studiosus inventi.[32]

It should be immediately noted that this analogy is a very difficult one to understand. To say that "divine light enkindles the feeble spark of the mind" is obviously a type of Neoplatonic and Augustinian expression, but what it actually means is very difficult to decipher because of the fact that there is a mixture of the referential value of two analogies here. Reference to "divine light" is itself an analogy. Reference to "the feeble spark of the mind" is another analogy. The statement then applies the first analogy to the second, with the result that an actual understanding of any conceptual content is almost impossible. What can perhaps be understood is that Boethius means, somehow, that the primary agency involved in his theological reflection is itself divine.

Now, with regard to these analogical images of: 1) a "divine light" that "enkindles," and 2) "the feeble spark" of the mind, the following interpretive points should be noted. To refer to "divine light" is a metaphor, for divine "light" cannot be corporeal light. Secondly, in the ancient world all light either literally came from fire, or was thought to come from fire, and thus it was quite natural to see "light" as being able to "enkindle." Thirdly, the reference to the "spark" of the human mind is an echo of Stoic and other themes. Now, the dilemma or tension which the present author sees in the combination of these metaphors in the manner proposed by Boethius is this: if the "feeble spark" of the human mind can actually be "enkindled" by the "divine light" (fire), then that which is received by the human mind would appear to be essentially the same type of thing as the divine "light" (fire), but this cannot be the case. What Boethius does not clarify in his briefly stated, double metaphor, is that the way in which the divine "light" (fire) "enkindles" the "feeble spark" of the human mind can only be by way of an increased

---

[32]   Boethius, Tractate I, *Trinitas Unus Deus Ac Non Tres Dii*, i.e., *De Trinitate* (p. 2). I have very long pondered this question, so far as the divine light has deemed it fitting to enkindle the feeble spark of my mind. Now, having set it forth in logical order and cast it into literary form, I have caused it to be presented and communicated to you, being as much desirous of your judgement as zealous for my own discovery.

[The above translation is mainly based on the 1973 revision in the Loeb edition by S. Tester. However, in one regard the translation of Tester is less adequate here than that in the earlier Loeb edition by Stewart. The key phrase, "quantum nostrae mentis igniculum lux divina dignata est," is translated by Tester as: "so far as the divine light has deemed it fitting for the spark of my intelligence to do so." This does not express well the complex analogy being used, let alone the difficulty of that analogy. The earlier translation by Stewart was: "to the extent that the divine light has deigned to enkindle the feeble spark of my mind." This better expresses the key idea. It should also be noted that the exact MS of Boethius which Aquinas had is not known.]

participation of the "spark" in the "light" (fire), without the attainment of the essence of the divine "light" itself. What is at work in Boethius' statement is a "mixture of metaphors" on the level of their referential value. There is not a mixture of metaphors on the literal level, there are only problems of meaning on the literal level. For example, in the corporeal order of "fire, "light," and a "feeble spark," one can easily imagine the case of smoldering embers, remnants of a large wooden fire that had burned all night. These smoldering embers would have lost their power to burst forth into flame, even though they were located in and around wood that could be brought to flame. Now, if a more powerful fire were to be joined to those embers, they could then regain their strength and bring to flame the burnable material around them. But what then results is an identity of essence of the external agent, the fire, and that which results from the reinforced action of the embers which were previously only weak "sparks" - fire. It is in this sense that there is a tension in the referential value of the two metaphors that Boethius here employs. However, at the same time, it must be acknowledged that Boethius does not say that the divine "light" (fire) can "inflame" his own mind; he merely says that it may "enkindle" the "spark" of his mind, and there does seem to be remotely implied in this phrasing a sort of participatory distance. The fundamental problem here is, of course, the limit-nature of revelation as far as human conceptuality is concerned; it is, again, the problem of mediation and participation verus immediacy - or mediation and participation *and* "immediacy." It may be that on a conceptual level of what Augustine would call "scientia" one is forced to an "either/or" decision; but that on a level of what Augustine would call "sapientia" one may formulate a "both/and" position. But rather than digressing to a lengthy discussion of this point - important as it is - based on only the first sentence of Tractate I, it would be best to continue a summary of the *De Trinitate.*

Boethius then immediately states that such secret and hidden doctrines as those of the Trinity are "only for the few," and that he discusses this topic only with John the Deacon. He has come not to discuss it with others, because he has found that he meets with only the apathy of the dullard or the jealously of the shrewd, who trample underfoot such hidden truths and thus seem to bring discredit on the study of divinity.[33] In order that this not happen with his written text, Boethius expressly states that he has shrouded his work in brevity, and with the use of very technical terms, which will prevent the rest of the world from bothering to read this Tractate. He also expresses his own critical consciousness of the limits of understanding possible in such an inquiry:

---

[33] Ibid. p. 4.

Sane tantum a nobis quaeri oportet quantum humanae rationis intuitus ad divinitatis valet celsa conscendere. Nam ceteris quoque artibus idem quasi quidam finis est constitutus, quousque potest via rationis accedere. Neque enim medicina aegris semper affert salutem; sed nulla erit culpa medentis, si nihil eorum quae fieri oportebat omiserit. Idemque in ceteris. At quantum haec difficilior quaestio est, tam facilior esse debet ad veniam. Vobis tamen etiam illud inspiciendum est, an ex beati Augustini scriptis semina rationum aliquos in nos venientia fructus extulerint. Ac de proposita quaestione hinc sumamus initium.[34]

Boethius then states his understanding of the true Trinitarian doctrine of the Catholic faith. His method is based principally on the authority of Augustine, and there are no references to biblical texts. The "Father," the "Son," and the "Holy Spirit" are each God, but they are one God and not three Gods. The reason for the unity as one God is, Boethius argues, the absence of difference and the absence of a kind of numerical plurality. His brevity in the exposition of these arguments in Section I of the Tractate does not draw the full conclusions; this happens only later in Section III, after a discussion of the methods in the sciences in Section II. In Section I he only argues that the principle of plurality is otherness, and the diversity of things lies in their difference according to genus, species, or number.[35] Likewise, identity can be predicated according to genus, species, or number, e.g., a man is the same as a horse in that they have the same genus, Cato is the same as Cicero in that they have the same species, and Tully is the same as Cicero in that they have the same number, i.e., one. Cato, Tully, and Cicero do not differ by genus or species, but by their accidents, such as the places which they occupy. And it is because of the difference in their accidents that Cato, Tully, and Cicero are plural in number. The actually unstated conclusion in this section is that numerical plurality cannot apply to the divine Persons of the Trinity, for they cannot differ in accidents.

---

[34]   Ibid. We should of course press our inquiry only so far as the insight of human reason is allowed to climb the height of divine knowledge. For in other arts the same point is set as a sort of limit, as far as which the way of reason can reach. Medicine, for example, does not always bring health to the sick, though the doctor will not be to blame if he has left nothing undone which should have been done. So too with the other arts. In the present case, the very difficulty of the quest claims that there should be a lenient judgement. You must, however, examine whether the "semina rationum" sown in my mind by St. Augustine's writings have borne fruit. And now let us make a beginning on the question proposed.

[Here the technical term "semina rationum" has been left as is rather than attempting to translate it. In the Loeb edition, S. Tester offers a translation as "seeds of argument," but this does away with the exceptionally rich, Neoplatonic nuances of "seminal reasons," which is key to the meaning in Augustine, and which would certainly have been well understood by Boethius, as well acquainted as he was not only with Augustine, but with Proclus as well.]

[35]   Here Boethius follows Aristotle, *Topics*, A7, 102b 6 ff.

In Section II, Boethius seems almost to begin again from the beginning, by stating the divisions of the sciences, a topic that will particularly occupy Aquinas in his own Questions 5 and 6 of his *Expositio*. Some historical context is necessary in order to appreciate the proposal of Boethius, and the analysis of Aquinas.

Both Boethius and Aquinas propose a three-fold division of the speculative sciences: physics, mathematics, and theology. This Boethian division is actually a quite common Neoplatonic theme.[36] In the Platonic tradition itself, there is a three-fold division of "being" into the things of the sensory domain, mathematical realities, and the Forms or Ideas themselves. In Aristotle, there is a three-fold division of the speculative sciences into natural sciences, mathematics, and theology (meaning metaphysics),[37] and this division is repeated in the *Commentary* on the *Metaphysics* attributed to Alexander of Aphrodisias.[38] Also of historical note is the fact that in the *Enneads* I, 3 of Plotinus, the first stage of education was to be music and mathematics, and then one could proceed to "dialectics." The meaning of such "dialectics" in Plotinus is, like most of Plotinian philosophy, very difficult to understand, but it is reasonable to say that by such "dialectics" Plotinus meant a process of "transcendental" and "metaphysical" consciousness. Plotinus was certainly well aware of Plato's views on "thinking" as an "inner dialogue of the soul," in which there was a process of asking questions, finding answers, and making both affirmations and denials, in the silence of one's own self.[39] In this Platonic and Plotinian viewpoint, "dialectic is inherent in the process of introspection, in the zigzag of contemplative ascent to the divine realm."[40] Since the Boethian project is precisely an attempted synthesis of Aristotelian and Platonic philosophy, one should well anticipate that the meaning of "transcendental" or "metaphysical" science, for Boethius, will involve a dialectical addition to Aristotelian processes of metaphysical reasoning, and that this structure will be repeated by Aquinas, in his own reflections on the nature of metaphysics, and, by extension, on the nature of sacred theology.

What Boethius proposes in Section II is that speculative science may be divided into natural philosophy (i.e., physics), mathematics, and theology (i.e., metaphysics). Physics deals with the forms of bodies which are in matter, and such forms cannot be separated in reality from matter. Mathematics deals with the forms of bodies considered apart from matter and therefore apart from motion, although these forms do not actually exist apart from matter and motion. Theology, however, deals with the divine substance, which exists apart from matter and motion. Following from the natures of the

---

36 Chadwick, *Boethius*, pp. 108-111.
37 Aristotle, *Metaphysics* E 1, 1026a 13-16.
38 Alexander of Aphrodisias, *Commentary on Metaphysics*, E 1.
39 Cf. Plato, *Republic*, 532a ff; *Theaetetus*, 189e-190a; and *Sophist*, 263e.
40 Chadwick, *Boethius*, p. 109.

objects to be considered, physics is to proceed "rationabiliter," or in a scientific process of reasoning; mathematics is to proceed "disciplinaliter," or in a systematic process of science; while theology is to proceed "intellectualiter," which means a purely intellectual process, which does not rely on the imagination, since the divine substance which is sought in theology is without both matter and motion. The divine substance is a pure form which cannot be imagined, and it is the source of all being rather than a being, and its very Being is identical with its own Essence.

At the end of Section II, Boethius makes the connection with Section I and the transition to Section III: since the Being of the divine substance is identical with the Essence of the divine substance, there can be no plurality arising out of difference, no multiplicity based on accidents, and there can be no number in the divine substance.

In Section III Boethius then asserts that God is absolutely identical with God, with no differences based on accidents. "Father," "Son," and "Holy Spirit" do not result in a plurality of number based on a difference in essence. And the fact that "God" can be predicated of "Father," "Son," and "Holy Spirit" does not result in a plurality of number, for there is no plurality of essence. At the same time, "Father," "Son," and "Holy Spirit" are not synonymous terms, for their meanings are not identical, even though their essence is one. There is not a complete indifference in the usage of the terms, but the type of difference is not one of essence.

In Section IV, Boethius then turns to the ten categories: substance, quality, quantity, relation, place, time, condition, situation, activity, and passivity. Boethius holds that these categories of predication can be applied to sensible things, but not to God.[41] "Relation" cannot be technically predicated of God, for God is not a substance related to other substances, but is supersubstantial, and thus cannot be "related to" any other substances in the ways that sensible substances are related to sensible substances. One may predicate terms of God. For example, one may say "God is just"; but the meaning is actually more than substantial predication versus the accidental predication that is found when one says "Socrates is just," because God is supersubstantial rather than substantial, and thus all predications of God are of a supersubstantial. But the meaningfulness of such predication cannot be grasped by finite consciousness, and all finite predications are thus inadequate, for each finite predication is a "this or that." Boethius alludes to this most fundamental problem of the distance between the finite and the infinite in his *Consolation of Philosophy:*

---

[41]   Here Boethius echoes Plotinus, *Enneads*, V, 5, 10; VI, 2, 3, 7; Augustine, *Confessions*, VI, 16, 28-29; *De Trinitate*, V, 8, 9; and Proclus, *In Parm.*, 1192, 1 ff. See discussion in Chadwick, *Boethius*, p. 216.

Omnem terrae ambitum, sicuti astrologicis demonstrationibus accepisti, ad caeli spatium puncti constat obtinere rationem, id est ut, si ad caelestis globi magnitudinem conferatur, nihil spatii prorsus habere iudicetur.[42]

In the same way, the scandal of metaphysical and theological discourse is that it technically seems to be able only to have "no size at all."

Now a particular problem is presented with the use of the term "relation" as applied to the Trinity. The basic rejection of Boethius of the predication of "relation" of God is in the sense of "relation" between two physical substances. In such a case, relation is an accident. For example, the relationship of a human father to a human son is accidental. But there can be no accidents in God. Indeed, for Boethius, God cannot properly be considered a "substance" which can be an "object" in any sense.

But, it is obvious that Augustinian Trinitarian theology makes use of the notion of "relation," in some manner of predication. And Boethius then turns in Section V to a discussion of this particular problem. Such a use of the term "relation" cannot mean relation to another substance, but only relation to another Person of the same Essence, and yet such a use of terms is hardly able to be understood.

Quocirca si pater ac filius ad aliquid dicuntur nihilque aliud ut dictum est differunt nisi sola relatione, relatio vero non praedicatur ad id de quo dicitur, non faciet alteritatem rerum de qua dicitur, sed, si dici potest, quo quidem modo id quod vix intellegi potuit interpretatum est, personarum.[43]

The distinction of "relation" within the divine substance cannot be based on an accidental difference, but only a type of relative difference which is basically impossible for finite consciousness to understand. This particular, theological predication of "relation" does not involve any spatial or corporeal distinction, and no distinction of essence, and thus no distinction of number; it is only a hardly understandable distinction of what is an essential unity without any real plurality. It is with this theme that Boethius finishes his Section V.

In his concluding Section VI, Boethius holds that divine "relation" can only be the "relation" of "identicals." Since "Father," "Son," and "Holy

---

[42]   Boethius, *Consolation of Philosophy*, II, 7 (Loeb Classical Library Edition, p. 212). You have learned from astronomical proofs that the whole circle of our earth is but a point in comparison with the extent of the whole heavens; that is, if it is compared in size with the celestial sphere, it is judged to have no size at all.

[43]   Boethius, Tractate I, *De Trinitate* (p. 26). Wherefore if 'Father' and 'Son' are predicates of relation, and, as we have said, have no other difference but that of relation, but relation is not predicated as if it were the thing itself and objectively predicated of it, it will not imply an otherness of the things of which it is said, but, in a phrase which aims at interpreting what we could hardly understand, an otherness of persons.

Spirit" are equals, of the same Essence, a Trinitarian Relation can only be a Relation of Identicals.

> Quod si id in cunctis aliis rebus non potest inveniri, facit hoc cognata caducis rebus alteritas. Nos vero nulla imaginatione diduci sed simplici intellectu erigi et ut quidque intellegi potest ita aggredi etiam intellectu oportet. [44]

This is the ultimate dialectical moment in theology. In the transitory nature of human experience in this world, nothing exactly like such a divine relation can be found, and all particularizing and limiting acts of the imagination must be negated. The pure and simple understanding which Boethius advocates as necessary is a type of final goal of non-limited consciousness, seemingly emancipated from the conditions of corporeal consciousness.[45]

Boethius concludes his Tractate I with a very subtle allusion, and a posture which reflects the priority of supplication in prayer rather than great confidence in the ability of finite reason to penetrate Absolute Mystery:

> Quod si sententiae fidei fundamentis sponte firmissimae opitulante gratia divina idonea argumentorum adiumenta praestitimus, illuc perfecti operis laetitia remeabit unde venit effectus. Quod si ultra se humanitas nequivit ascendere, quantum inbecillitas subtrahit vota supplebunt.[46]

Boethius seems to mean here that theological reflection on the mystery of the Trinity occurs only with the aid of divine grace. The ultimate cause of finite theological reflection is God himself, in an "exitus-reditus" pattern that is part of the mysterious and providential plan of salvation. While human nature and human reason cannot adequately sense or understand this, it is, still vaguely, "sensed" and "understood" in contemplation. There is no great confidence in the *De Trinitate* of Boethius about the ability of even graced-reason to formulate understandable propositions about the Trinity. The "first of the scholastics" thus differs from the actual practice of most of the "Neoscholasticism" of the "thomistic" commentators. The dialectical tension in Boethian theology is more explicitly profound than even in most texts of

---

[44]   Ibid. (p. 30). But if a relation of this kind cannot be found in all other things, this is because of the otherness natural to all perishable, transitory objects. But we ought not to be led astray by imagination, but raised up by pure understanding and, so far as anything can be understood, to this point also we should approach it with our understanding.

[45]   Cf. Augustine, *De Trinitate*, esp. Book 10, Chapters 8 and 11, for his warnings that one must purge the mind of notions of size, space, and all bodily images, although this is extremely difficult to achieve.

[46]   Boethius, Tractate I, *De Trinitate* (p. 30). If, by the grace of God helping me, I have furnished some fitting support in argument to an article which stands quite firmly by itself on the foundations of faith, the joy felt for the finished work will flow back to the source from which its effecting came. But if human nature has failed to reach beyond its limits, whatever my weakness takes away, my prayers will make up.

Aquinas. The relationship between faith and reason in Boethius is one of an extremely cautious acknowledgement of some possibility of the necessary reconciliation of the two domains. At the conclusion of his Tractate II, Boethius stated only that *insofar as possible*, faith and reason might be reconciled. The tendency in Aquinas, for complex historical reasons arising from Latin Averroism, will be to insist on a much cleaner reconciliation than may well be possible for human reason and faith. In all the central mysteries of the faith, rational understanding only arrives at a limit-point, which cannot be crossed, and at this point two contradictories are presented, and it is the act of faith which then dialectically negates the contradiction in an act that is "above reason." Boethius' boldly intellectual faith faced this paradox much more honestly than Aquinas' historical situation would allow his to do.

> Quaenam discors foedera rerum
> Causa resolvit? Quis tanta deus
> Veris statuit bella duobus,
> Ut quae carptim singula constent.
> Eadem nolint mixta iugari?[47]

The Influence of the Tractates

As to the role of these theological tractates of Boethius in the medieval program of studies, it is possible that Alcuin had expounded the *Opuscula Sacra* of Boethius to his pupils at Aachen.[48] The theological tractates seem to have first appeared as a school text as such in the early 9th century, often bound together with *De Consolatione Philosophiae*. Hincmar, Archbishop of Rheims (845-882), one of the most influential churchmen of his time, was particularly fond of the theological tractates of Boethius, and cited them along with Augustine, Jerome, Ambrose, Gregory, and Bede in order to weight the authority of his arguments.[49] And at this point the theological writings of Boethius became standard texts, available in any good library and used by scholars with an increasing familiarity. John Scotus Eriugena made

---

[47] Boethius, *Consolation of Philosophy*, V, 3 (Loeb Classical Library Edition, p. 403). The following translation is from the Loeb edition by Tester.
What cause discordant breaks the world's compact?
What god sets strife so great
Between two truths,
That those same things which stand, alone and separate,
Together mixed, refuse to be so yoked?
[48] M. Gibson, "The *Opuscula Sacra* in the Middle Ages," in *Boethius: His Life, Thought and Influence*, p. 215.
[49] See, e.g., Hincmar of Rheims, *De una et non trina deitate*, PL 125, 473C-618B. This work, written ca. 853-860 as an attack against the position of Gottschalk, cites the *Opuscula Sacra* some thirty times.

frequent use of them, and the *Sic et Non* of Peter Abelard rested principally
on Augustine and Boethius for its fundamental Trinitarian positions.[50] But in
Abelard one finds the use of Boethius simply as a source for proof texts; there
is not a real entry into the questions. And Peter Lombard's *Sentences* treated
the Boethian writings in the same manner. In 12th-century Paris these
theological tractates were usually studied in the general context of "sentence
literature" loci for dialectics, and were repeatedly utilized by major
commentators on Peter Lombard. Both Alexander of Hales and Hugh of St.
Cher, himself a Dominican master at Paris (1230-1235), made frequent use of
Boethius in their commentaries on the *Sentences*.[51] In one sense, Aquinas was
part of this tradition - but with the important difference that he not only
lectured on the *Sentences*, using Boethius, he subsequently engaged the
theological tractates directly, giving to them the status of more independent
texts, worthy of serving as a point of departure for Aquinas' own thought.[52] In
the 12th century both the *De Trinitate* and the *De Hebdomadibus* were also
treated in actual commentaries by the early schoolmen, with some 20
commentaries written on the *De Trinitate* alone between 1120 and 1200.[53]
The particular energy invested in such commentary in the 12th century was
most likely due to the intense interest in the methodology of Boethius which,
while making no use of Sacred Scripture as such, explored the rational
foundations of Trinitarian theology in a manner quite attractive to the
"dialecticians." But Aquinas was the only major 13th-century philosopher or
theologian to comment upon the tractates.[54] A great advance in the treatment
of the Boethian theological tractates was made by Gilbert de la Porrée in the
mid-12th century. Gilbert was concerned with precise theological method and
with bringing theological discussion of the Trinity to the intellectual level of

---

[50] See, e.g., Peter Abelard, *Sic et Non*, VIII-IX; PL 177, 1359D-66D, which cites Tractate I
at 1360D-62A, 1364D-5A. See also B. Boyer and R. McKeon, *Peter Abailard* (Chicago:
University of Chicago Press, 1976), II, pp. 130-136.
[51] See discussion in W. Principe, *Hugh of Saint-Cher's Theology of the Hypostatic Union*.
Studies and Texts XIX (Toronto: Pontifical Institute of Mediaeval Studies, 1970).
[52] Cf. Gibson, "The *Opuscula Sacra* in the Middle Ages," p. 229; J. Weisheipl, *Friar
Thomas d'Aquino: His Life, Thought, and Work* (Garden City: Doubleday, 1974), p. 134.
[53] See discussion in L. Elders, *Faith and Science: An Introduction to St. Thomas' 'Expositio
in Boethii De Trinitate.'* Studia Universitatis S. Thomae in Urbe (Rome: Herder, 1974), pp. 13-
15. See also G. Schrimpf, *Die Axiomenschrift des Boethius (de Hebdomadibus) als
Philosophisches Lehrbuch des Mittelalters* (Leiden: Brill, 1966); G. Evans, "More Geometrico:
The Place of the Axiomatic Method in the Twelfth-Century Commentaries on Boethius'
Opuscula Sacra," *Archives Internationales d'histoire des sciences* 27 (1977) 207-221.
[54] There may have been one other 13th-century commentary on the *De Trinitate* by a certain
Helye, of the Faculty of Arts of the University of Paris, but this disputed work may actually have
been written in the 12th century. The claimed manuscript of this commentary, which was said to
have been in Codex 382 of the Stiftsbibliotek at Admont, disappeared. See discussion in S.
Neumann, *Gegenstand und Methode der theoretischen Wissenschaften nach Thomas von Aquin
auf Grund der Expositio super librum Boethii de Trinitate* (Münster: Aschendorff, 1965), p. 8.

the best contemporary work in logic.[55] This attempt at some intellectual clarity met with strong conservative opposition, but within twenty years of Gilbert's death his *Commentary* on the *Opuscula Sacra* was accepted as definitive. Nevertheless, in the 13th century neither the *Opuscula Sacra* themselves nor the *Commentary* of Gilbert was a standard text either at Paris or at other universities, and it seems that Aquinas was the only major 13th-century thinker to attempt a thorough study and entry into these Boethian tractates.

---

[55] See N. Häring, ed., *The Commentaries on Boethius by Gilbert of Poitiers*. Studies and Texts XIII (Toronto: Pontifical Institute of Mediaeval Studies, 1966). See also N. Häring, ed., *Commentaries on Boethius by Thierry of Chartres and His School* (Toronto: Pontifical Institute of Mediaeval Studies, 1971).

CHAPTER THREE

AQUINAS: THE *EXPOSITIO* OF THE *DE TRINITATE*

The Date of the Expositio

As will be seen, it is more fitting to call Aquinas' exploration of the *De Trinitate* an "expositio" rather than a "commentary," because Aquinas goes far beyond the limits of mere commentary in this work.[1] He actually uses Boethius as a point of departure for his own systematic theology.

The exact date and circumstances surrounding Aquinas' *Expositio* are very debated in the literature, but some reasonable conclusions can be formulated. At one extreme is the position of Bonnefroy, for whom the *Expositio* was actually written *after* the *Summa Theologiae*.[2] Since the *Summa Theologiae* (1266-1273) is itself incomplete, it is hard to see how Aquinas could have begun or attempted to finish another major project *after* this, since his health and motivation for writing had drastically changed in 1273. At the same time, when one looks at the relative sophistication of the *Expositio* and the methodological reflections of the *Summa Theologiae*, one cannot but regard the former work as more "mature." If it is actually an earlier work, one must account for this difference. But this can be easily enough be accounted for simply by noting the two very different purposes of these two works. In the *Expositio*, Aquinas was freely exploring his own way of thought, while in the

---

[1]   Aquinas, *Expositio Super Librum Boethii De Trinitate*, ed. B. Decker (Leiden: Brill, 1955, repr. with corrections, 1959, 1965). This is the critical edition and all references will be to the 1965 edition, with page numbers in Decker in parentheses. See also discussion in P.-M. Gils, "L'édition Decker du 'In Boethium de Trinitate' et les autographs de s. Thomas d'Aquin," *Scriptorium* 10 (1956) 111-120, and his [Notes on the 1959 edition] *Bulletin thomiste* 11 (1960-1961) 41-44. The partial edition of P. Wyser, *In librum Boethii De Trinitate Quaestiones quinta et sexta* (Fribourg and Louvain: Societé philosophique, 1948), was based on Autograph Cod. Vat. Lat. 9850 and was not a fully critical edition based on all the manuscript evidence. There are English translations published in A. Maurer, *Thomas Aquinas: Faith, Reason and Theology* [Qq. 1-4] and A. Maurer, *The Division and Methods of the Sciences* [Qq. 5-6], 4th ed. (Toronto: Pontifical Institute of Mediaeval Studies, 1986). Maurer has been consulted, but all English translations here are those of the present author.
[2]   J.-F. Bonnefroy, "La théologie comme science et l'explication de la foi selon saint Thomas d'Aquin," *Ephemerides Theologicae Louvanienses* 14 (1937), 421-446.

Summa Theologiae he clearly at least began the project with the goal of addressing only students still in the early years of their theological studies.

Another extreme position in the literature, also poorly reasoned, is that the *Expositio* was actually begun before Aquinas *started* writing the *Commentary on the Sentences*, which is incorrectly dated by some as 1256.[3] Both Neumann and Elders actually support this interpretation.[4] One basis for this view is that the letter of Pope Alexander IV to the Chancellor of the University of Paris praising the University for having given Aquinas the position of *magister (licentiam in theologia facultate docendi)* was dated March 3, 1256. But the *Bulla* of Alexander ordering that the University grant Aquinas his full rights as a *magister* was later issued on October 23, 1256, leading one to believe that Aquinas had not yet been admitted to actually teaching at the University. The question then is: "what was Aquinas doing between March and October of 1256?" Neumann and Elders propose that Aquinas began working on the *Expositio*, then *began* the *Commentary on the Sentences* in November of 1256, and then returned to work on the *Expositio* when the *Commentary* was finished. But here, while both both Neumann and Elders are correct that Aquinas began his *Expositio* of the *De Trinitate* after March of 1256, and while they are correct that Aquinas worked on revisions of his *Commentary on the Sentences* after March of 1256, their view that the *Expositio* was finished *before* the *Commentary on the Sentences* is absolutely incorrect. The present study agrees with Weisheipl, that the *Commentary on the Sentences* was completed in its initial version by March of 1256, and that while Aquinas did engage in later revisions, these were never fully completed. The present study acknowledges that the complex problems of dating the various manuscripts and sections of the *Commentary on the Sentences* have still not been resolved, but it would be stretching matters far beyond the available evidence to hold that the *Expositio* was finished *before* the substantial version of the *Commentary*, as it is now available in the editions, was finished.

A more reasonable position is that of Chenu, who discovered that Annibaldo d'Annibaldi used some of Aquinas' unfinished *Expositio* of the *De Trinitate* in his own brief *Commentary on the Sentences*, which Annibaldo

---

[3]   The dating of this *Commentary* is debated. For the definitive argumentation that this *Commentary* was begun in 1252, see Weisheipl, *Friar Thomas d'Aquino*.

[4]   Neumann, *Gegenstand und Methode der theoretischen Wissenschaften nach Thomas von Aquin auf Grund der Expositio super librum Boethii de Trinitate*, pp. 7ff; Elders, *Faith and Science: An Introduction to St. Thomas' 'Expositio in Boethii De Trinitate,'* pp. 19-20. Elders holds that a careful comparison of the *Commentary on the Sentences* and the *Expositio* "shows that there is nothing which proves that the *Scriptum* is older, whereas on a few occasions there is an indication that the EBT was written first" (p. 20). But in general, one cannot but note the great difference in levels of sophistication that distinguishes the two works. The best historical evidence also shows that Aquinas would have started his *Commentary on the Sentences* before he started the *Expositio*. In instances where sections of the *Commentary* seem quite mature, this may simply be due to the fact that they are later revisions.

completed while lecturing on the *Sentences* in Paris, with Aquinas as his master.[5] For Chenu, Annibaldo lectured on the *Sentences* in the period 1258-1260, and probably finished writing his *Commentary* shortly thereafter. Chenu and Eschmann date this *Commentary* of Annibalo as finished around 1260-1261, and hold that Aquinas' *Expositio* was likely completed by 1258, or 1260 at the latest.[6]

What is clear is that Aquinas' also incomplete *Expositio in Librum Boethii De Hebdomadibus* parallels the themes of the *Expositio* of the *De Trinitate*, and the level of treatment shows that these two works should be dated at around the same period. Weisheipl dates this other, unfinished *Expositio* as 1256-1259.[7] For Wyser, the *Expositio* of the *De Trinitate* can also be dated 1255-1259.[8] Grabmann and Mandonnet date it 1257-1258.[9]

Synave dates the work in question at 1256, at the beginning of Aquinas' period as a master in Paris, with the 24 articles being 24 "disputed questions" held in the 12 weeks from April 24th to July 21st.[10] Corbin agrees with the argumentation of Synave as well as with the date of 1256.[11] But both Synave and Corbin seem to ignore the problem that the *Expositio* does not follow the non-integrated thematic sequence of "disputed questions," and thus their argumentation collapses in this regard. This is aside from the fact that it is hard to imagine how Aquinas could have possibly formulated the extremely sophisticated reflections of the *Expositio* in a brief, 12-week period, between April and July of 1256. Synave and Corbin do note the parallel themes of Question 3, Article 1 of the *Expositio* of the *De Trinitate* and Question 14, Article 10 of the *De Veritate*. They also find that the solution in the *De Veritate* text is much more clear and developed than in the *Expositio*. Thus they conclude that the *De Veritate* text is of a later date, and this is a justified conclusion. Synave and Corbin date the later *De Veritate* Question 14, in the

---

[5]   Annibaldo d'Annibaldi wrote a *Commentary on the Sentences* in Paris, ca. 1258-1260. For centuries it was assumed that this *Commentary* had actually been written by Aquinas, and it is published in *Opera Omnia S. Thomae Aquinatis*, Vivès Edition, vol. 30.

[6]   I. Eschmann, "A Catalogue of St. Thomas' Works: Bibliographical Notes," in E. Gilson, *The Christian Philosophy of St. Thomas Aquinas* (New York: Random House, 1956), pp. 381-439, esp. p. 406, fn40; M.-D. Chenu, "La date du commentaire de saint Thomas sur le *De Trinitate* de Boèce," *Les sciences philosophiques et théologiques* 30 (1941/1942), 432-434; *La théologie comme science au XIIIe siècle* (Paris: Desclée, 1957), p. 81. Chenu finds that Annibaldo implicitly quotes from Aquinas' *Expositio* (q. 2, a. 2, ad 7) in his own *Commentary* (I, q. 1, a. 1, ad 2).

[7]   Weisheipl, *Friar Thomas d'Aquino*, p. 382.

[8]   Wyser, ed., *In librum Boethii De Trinitate Quaestiones quinta et sexta*, pp. 14-18.

[9]   M. Grabmann, *Die Werke des hl. Thomas von Aquin* (Münster: Aschendorff, 1931), pp. 18-21. P. Mandonnet, *Des écrits authentiques de saint Thomas d'Aquin*, 2nd ed. rev. and corrected (Fribourg: S. Paul, 1910), p. 153.

[10]   P. Synave, "La révélation des vérités divines naturelles d'après saint Thomas," *Mélanges Mandonnet: études d'histoire litteraire et doctrinale du moyen âge*, vol. 1 (Paris: Vrin, 1930), pp. 327-365.

[11]   Corbin, *Le chemin de la théologie chez Thomas d'Aquin*, p. 298.

early part of the academic year 1257-1258, and this is also justifiable, though not yet demonstrable. Synave's reason for this dating is that he holds this was the time for the *Quaestiones Disputatae* 9-20.[12] Synave seems to have based his dating of Question 14 on Mandonnet. The academic year 1257-1258 was the period assigned by Mandonnet for the *Quaestiones Disputatae* 9-20.[13] But a devastating criticism of this dating by Mandonnet was provided by Dondaine, who pointed out the clumsy impossibility of dividing articles within a single disputed question into different academic years, and this criticism was then repeated by Weisheipl.[14] Glorieux tried to revise Mandonnet's basic position and avoid the problem of having to separate articles within a single question into different academic years, but still did not fully solve the problem of dating the *Quaestiones Disputatae*.[15] Although Weisheipl[16] disagrees with some of Mandonnet's dating, Weisheipl does date questions 8-20 of *De Veritate* in the academic year 1257-1258. Thus, since sections of Question 14 of the *De Veritate* parallel Question 3, Article 1 of the *Expositio*, and present a more sophisticated and mature treatment, one can reasonably argue that this Article of the *Expositio* was finished before 1257, but this does not mean that one can conclude, with Synave, that the entire *Expositio* was finished in 1256.

The most reasonable conclusion that can be reached at present is simply that all that Aquinas wrote for his unfinished *Expositio* of the *De Trinitate* was written after the basic work on the *Scriptum super libros Sententiarum* (1252-1256), at about the same time as the *Expositio in librum Boethii de Hebdomadibus* (1256-1259?), and before the *Summa Contra Gentiles* (1259-1264), thus the *Expositio* was most likely written in the period 1256-1259.[17]

The Motivation of the Expositio

It is most probable that Aquinas first studied Boethius at the University of Naples and at the Dominican *studium generale* at Naples, during his five years of formation in the arts and philosophy (1239-1244).[18] His course of

---

[12]   P. Synave, "Le problème chronologique des questions disputées de s. Thomas d'Aquin," *Revue thomiste* 31 (1926), 156-159.

[13]   P. Mandonnet, "Introduction" to *Quaestiones Disputatae*, ed. P. Mandonnet (Paris: Lethielleux, 1925).

[14]   A. Dondaine, *Les secrétaires de s. Thomas*, 2 vols. (Rome: Leonine Commission, 1956); cited by Weisheipl, *Friar Thomas d'Aquino*, pp. 123-128.

[15]   P. Glorieux, "Les quaestiones disputatae de s. Thomas," *Recherches de théologie ancienne et médiévale* 4 (1932), 22.

[16]   Weisheipl, *Friar Thomas d'Aquino*, pp. 123-128, 362-363.

[17]   Cf. Decker, ed., "Prolegomena," in *Sancti Thomae de Aquino, Expositio Super Librum Boethii De Trinitate*, p. 44, who dates it in the period 1255-1259, while Weisheipl, *Friar Thomas d'Aquino*, pp. 381-382, 469 dates it 1253-1258.

[18]   Weisheipl, *Frair Thomas d'Aquino*, pp. 13ff.

studies at Naples would have followed the usual pattern of medieval universities of the period, except that in addition to the seven liberal arts, he also studied the natural philosophy of Aristotle, and this at a time when Parisian students were still forbidden to study Aristotle's natural philosophy and metaphysics.[19] At Naples, it is most likely that Aquinas studied the commentaries of Boethius on Aristotle's *Organon*, as well as the text of Boethius for arithmetic, and the *Musica* of Boethius for music and harmonic theory.[20] It is unlikely that Aquinas studied the theological tractates of Boethius in Napels; he may have begun such study under Albert the Great in Cologne.

Exactly why, around fifteen years after his first exposure to Boethius, Aquinas undertook expositions on the *De Trinitate* and the *De Hebdomadibus* is not agreed upon by scholars. For Weisheipl:

> There is no indication why Thomas chose to write commentaries on these two Boethian tractates. Possibly they were private lectures given at Saint-Jacques, but that does not seem likely. It is also possible that someone asked for clarification of these two tractates, and that Thomas obliged him with a short commentary. In any case, these two commentaries show the development of Thomas' thought during this early period at Paris.[21]

The structure and content of the *Expositio* of the *De Trinitate* are quite detailed and complex, and thus it is unlikely that the goal of Aquinas was a short commentary. The work is also clearly unfinished, and was to be part of a larger project. It is also the case that in the period 1256-1259, Aquinas was still a somewhat young theologian, at least chronologically, but in undertaking this *Expositio* he was attempting, at the age of 31-34, what was to be one of the most difficult and original projects of his theological career. And although Aquinas was still young at this time, the influence of the Boethian theological tractates was not a transitional one of his youth. Both the *De Hebdomadibus* of Boethius and the commentaries of Avicenna were used as starting points for Aquinas' own mature distinction of *esse* and *quid est*, and Boethius was particularly influential on Aquinas' development of his own doctrine of being, goodness, truth (and all the "transcendentals") *per*

---

[19]   On status of Aristotle in Paris, see *Chartularium Universitatis Parisiensis*, vol. 1, ed. H. Denifle and E. Châtelain (Paris: Delalain, 1889), pp. 78-80.

[20]   The works of Boethius, *Elements of Arithmetic*, *Elements of Music*, and *Elements of Geometry* (ca. 500-510) were summarizations of existing works by Nicomachus of Gersa and Euclid. Boethius also wrote two commentaries on the *Introduction* of Porphyry, a commentary on the *Categories* of Aristotle and a commentary on the *Topics* of Cicero.

[21]   Weisheipl, *Friar Thomas d'Aquino*, p. 138. See also Maurer, *Thomas Aquinas: Faith, Reason and Theology*, p. vii, who simply states that it is "plausible" that the *Expositio* can be dated in early 1256, while Aquinas may have been teaching at the Dominican Priory, Saint-Jacques, but Maurer admits that the exact circumstances are unknown. One may clearly see that the *Expositio* was not intended to be a short commentary and it was too advanced for beginning students.

essentiam as distinct from *per participationem*. It is also clearly the case that from the time of his early "Prologue" to his *Commentary on the Sentences*, Aquinas had a profound interest in the relationship of the Trinitarian processions to creation, incarnation, grace, and beatific vision, and a profound interest in the way these mysteries could be theologically understood in a mode of *sapientia*. Thus the unfinished project on the *De Trinitate* may have been an initial attempt to reach a systematic ordering and synthetic consideration of the grounds of theological methodology and the limited understanding of the Trinitarian mystery that is possible with a philosophy of metaphysical participation, analogy, and transcendental structure. Rather than being a small, transitional work, the *Expositio* of the *De Trinitate* is actually an unfinished, major work, of tremendous importance.

If the tractates were originally unified in the intentionality of Boethius as integrated components of a "single" project in Trinitarian theology, this is of some interest in that Aquinas worked on his expositions of the *De Trinitate* and the *De Hebdomadibus* at the same time (ca. 1256-1259). And one may speculate that Aquinas' motivation was an integrated treatment of participation, analogy, transcendental thematics, method, and Trinitarian theology. The original unity of the tractates and the significance of Aquinas' unfinished, integrative project is seriously overlooked in Weisheipl's *Friar Thomas d'Aquino*, even though it is a work of admittedly biographical focus. For Weisheipl:

> Before Thomas left Paris, he wrote an exposition on Boethius' *De trinitate* and *De hebdomadibus*, two anomalous and almost anachronistic works. These two treatises by Boethius are the second and third of his five theological tractates.[22]

It would be best to revise Weisheipl's ordering of the tractates. The *De Trinitate* and the *De Hebdomadibus* are actually Tractates I and III, as has been argued. And rather than seeing them as "anomalous and almost anachronistic works," it would be better to regard them as major, synthetic attempts at an intellectual understanding of Christian mysteries, which Aquinas regarded as rigorous theological masterpieces.[23] Aquinas indicates his own understanding of the larger structural relationships of the Boethian tractates in a comment he makes in his own "Prologue":

> Materia siquidem huius operis est in una divina essentia trinitas personarum … . Eius namque doctrina in tres partes dividitur. Prima namque est de trinitate personarum, ex quarum processione omnis alia

---

[22]   Weisheipl, *Friar Thomas d'Aquino*, p. 134.
[23]   Maurer, "Introduction," *Thomas Aquinas: Faith, Reason and Theology*, is more sensitive to this.

nativitas vel processio derivatur, in hoc quidem libro, qui prae manibus habetur, quantum ad id quod de trinitate et unitate sciendum est, in alio vero libro, quem ad Iohannem diaconum ecclesiae Romanae scribit, de modo praedicandi, quo utimur in personarum trinitate, qui sic incipit: *Quaero, an pater*. Secunda vero pars est de processione bonarum creaturarum a deo bono in libro, qui ad eundum Iohannem conscribitur *De hebdomadibus*, qui sic incipit: 'Postulas a me.' Tertia vero pars est de reparatione creaturarum per Christum. Quae quidem in duo dividitur. Primo namque proponitur fides, quam Christus docuit qua iustificamur, in libro qui intitulatur *De fide Christiana*, qui sic incipit: 'Christianam fidem.' Secundo explanatur, quid de Christo sentiendum sit, quomodo scilicet duae naturae in una persona conveniant, et hoc in libro *De duabus naturis in una persona Christi* ad Iohannem praedictum conscripto, qui sic incipit: 'Anxie te quidem.'[24]

The point here is that Aquinas indicates his awareness of the integration of the themes in all five of the Boethian tractates, and thus his concern should be seen as comprehensive.

The motivation of Aquinas seems to have been a continuation of "renaissance," 12th-century, dialectical theology as part of his own movement toward a new synthesis. This project of Aquinas should not be regarded as a throwback to the previous century, but a continuation of development. The influence of Boethius upon the early scholastic period (ca. 1000-1150) was so great that it could surely be called a "Boethian Age" as much as an "Aristotelian" one.[25] The Boethian project of Aquinas was an undertaking of some of the unfinished agenda of the 12th-century scholasticism of Gilbert de la Porrée and perhaps of the 13th-century agenda of Hugh of St. Cher and Albert the Great.

---

[24] Aquinas, "Prologue," *Expositio Super Librum Boethii de Trinitate* (Decker, pp. 46-47). The matter of this work is the Trinity of Persons in the one, divine Essence … . The teaching of Boethius on this is divided into three parts. The first part, concerning the Trinity of Persons, from whose procession every other nativity and procession are derived, is contained in that book which we have at hand [Tractate I: *De Trinitate*], which addresses what is to be known about the Trinity and unity. But in another book, which he wrote to John, a deacon of the church of Rome, [Boethius writes about] the mode of predication which is utilized [in speaking about] the persons of the Trinity, and this book begins with the words, 'I inquire whether father' [Tractate II]. The second part, which is about the procession of good creatures from a good God, is in a book which is written to the same John, 'De hebdomadibus,' [Tractate III], which begins with 'You ask of me.' The third part is about the restitution of creatures through Christ. This is divided into two sections. First there is set forth the faith which Christ taught and through which we are justified, in the book which is entitled, *De fide Christiana*, which begins, 'The Christian faith' [Tractate IV]. In the second section it is explained what is to be held concerning Christ, such as two natures in one person, and this is in the book, *De duabus naturis in una persona Christi*, written to the same John, which begins with the words, 'Anxie te quidem' [Tractate V: *A Treatise Against Eutyches and Nestorius*].

[25] See discussions in E. Rand, *The Founders of the Middle Ages* (Cambridge: Harvard University Press, 1928), and Gibson, ed., *Boethius: His Life, Thought, and Influence*, and H. Liebeschütz, "Boethius and the Legacy of Antiquity," in *The Cambridge History of Later Greek and Early Medieval Philosophy*, ed. A. Armstrong (Cambridge: Cambridge University Press, 1967).

The *De Trinitate* of Boethius is a brief work, occupying only four pages in the Migne edition.[26] But it was also the work of a master logician trying to adapt some of the technical notions of Aristotle so that Trinitarian theology could establish dogmatic propositions in accord with some rules of predication. It was Boethius who would have a lasting influence on Western Trinitarian theology because of his definition of "person" as "naturae rationabilis individua substantia,"[27] and his theory of relation: "substantia continet unitatem, relatio multiplicat trinitatem; atque ideo sola singillatim proferuntur atque separatim quae relationis sunt."[28] Aquinas was interested in Boethius as a master of method, particularly with regard to the use of reason *as well as* the "authorities." It is actually this type of theological method, in which systematic understanding presumes "the authorities" and then searches for intelligibility, which Aquinas himself practiced and which has more recently been proposed by Lonergan as the proper mode for systematics.[29] Aquinas himself notes the distinction between proceeding merely "by authorities" and proceeding "by reason" but presupposing the authorities in his own "Prologue" to the *Expositio*:

> Modus autem de trinitate tractandi duplex est, ut dicit Augustinus in I De trinitate, scilicet per auctoritates et per rationes, quem utrumque modum Augustinus complexus est, ut ipsemet dicit. Quidam vero sanctorum patrum, ut Ambrosius et Hilarius, alterum tantum modum prosecuti sunt, scilicet per auctoritates. Boethius vero elegit prosequi per alium modum, scilicet per rationes, praesupponens hoc quod ab aliis per auctoritates fuerat prosecutum.[30]

---

[26]   PL 64.

[27]   Boethius, Tractate V, *Contra Eutychen et Nestorium*, III (p. 84). The phrasing is slightly different in Migne, *De Duabus Naturis*, c. 3, PL 64.

[28]   Boethius, Tractate I, *De Trinitate*, VI (pp. 28-29; cf. Migne edition, PL 64, 1255 A). The substance preserves the unity, the relation makes up the Trinity; hence only terms belonging to relation may be applied singly and separately.

[29]   Lonergan, *Method in Theology*. Cf. M. Grabmann, *Die theologische Erkenntnis- und Einleitungslehre des hl. Thomas von Aquin auf Grund seiner Schrift 'In Boethium de Trinitate,' im Zusammenhang der Scholastik des 13. und beginnenden 14. Jahrhunderts dargestellt* (Freiburg: Paulusverlag, 1948).

[30]   Aquinas, "Prologue," *Expositio Super Librum Boethii de Trinitate* (pp. 47-48). There are two modes of treating the Trinity, as Augustine says in I *De Trinitate* [2], namely, by means of the authorities and by means of reasons, and Augustine used both of these modes in his treatment, as he himself says. Some of the fathers of the Church, such as Ambrose and Hilary, prescribed only one mode, namely that according to the authorities. Boethius however prescribes another mode, namely to proceed by means of reason, but presupposing that which had already been prescribed by those who used the method of proceeding by means of the authorities.

[See also discussion in Corbin, *Le chemin de la théologie chez Thomas d'Aquin*, pp. 294-295; cf. Aquinas, *Quaestiones Quodlibetales* IV, q. 9, a. 3.]

The point of interest here for Aquinas is a limited understanding, involving reason but not purely of reason, of the mysteries of the faith - an understanding, a limited intelligibility, following upon the acceptance of revelation.

The Structure of the Expositio

In this *Expositio*, Aquinas has come to a certain maturity after his four years (1252-1256) as a *Sententiarius* at Paris. The basic structure of the *Expositio* consists of: 1) an initial biblical reflection-meditation, on Wisdom 6,24, similar in style and purpose to Aquinas' opening meditation introducing his *Commentary on the Sentences*, 2) a more Aristotelian commentary and analysis of the "Preface" of Boethius, and 3) a shift in genre to six systematic questions which take their point of departure from the Boethian text, and which have four articles each. The structure of the six questions seems to point in a certain direction, but one must recall that the *Expositio* is an unfinished work, and thus one can only try to anticipate what Aquinas' full intentions were. In order to estimate those intentions, while it is helpful to attempt a projection from the Boethian text itself, since it is only being used by Aquinas as a point of departure, one has to look at the movement of the themes in Aquinas' own articulated questions, which clearly constitute more of an exploration and expansion of Boethian themes than a mere "commentary." These six systematic questions (themes) that Aquinas proposes are:

1) Human knowledge of divine things.
2) The manifestation of this knowledge of divine things.
3) The relationship of faith and the human person.
4) The cause of diversity and plurality.
5) The division of the speculative sciences.
6) The methods of the speculative sciences.

The structural sequence of the themes is of particular interest in that in this *Expositio* Aquinas is able to formulate his own sequence, at an advanced level, in a way he would not be able to do in either the *Summa Contra Gentiles* or the *Summa Theologiae*. It has traditionally been noted, e.g., by Weisheipl, that there is something of a methodological shift between questions 1-3 and questions 5 and 6, for the first three questions are clearly theological, and concerned with what may be termed *sacra doctrina;* while questions 5 and 6 are more philosophical considerations of the relationships and methods of the speculative sciences, i.e., in this case "physics," "mathematics," and "metaphysics." Between these two major groups of questions, Question 4, on "diversity and plurality," is practically never treated in the theological literature, and its strangeness is thus hardly recognized.[31] Question 4 is an analysis of the notion of "plurality" as it could apply to the Trinity of divine Persons. It is an example of the use of philosophy in Aquinas' theological methodology, but it does not contain explicit reflections on the nature of theological methodology. Since the *Expositio* is unfinished, one can only anticipate that Aquinas' intention was to continue the work beyond Question 6, with an explicit reflection on the Trinitarian mystery. But after one considers what Aquinas actually does in Questions 4, 5, and 6, one may well sense why the work was unfinished. The missing transition and completion of the work would be exceptionally difficult to accomplish.

What should also be immediately noted in the above sequence of themes in the six questions, is that this unfinished *Expositio* would have been the only major work of Aquinas to sequentially treat the precise methodology of metaphysics and then to treat the precise methodology of a systematic Trinitarian theology. Unfortunately, it is this ending section that was never completed by Aquinas. Somewhat amazingly, there is almost a complete absence in the literature of any attempts to speculate on what the completed *Expositio* could have looked like with a properly theological conclusion. There are, in fact, very few theological studies of this work, in part because of the relatively recent completion of the critical Latin edition, and in part because of the difficulty of analyzing the work.

Most studies of the *Expositio* have focused on a philosophical analysis of Questions 5 and 6;[32] particularly with regard to the importance of the negative judgement of *separatio* which yields intellectual knowledge that being is not limited to material being, and which negative judgement is not an "abstraction" of being. However, the full implications of this negative judgement in metaphysics for the status of theological language are not drawn out by Aquinas in this unfinished work, and these implications are also not generally treated in the literature.[33]

---

[31]   Here Maurer, "Introduction," *Thomas Aquinas: Faith, Reason and Theology*, esp. pp. xxiii-xxxv, is a refreshing exception.

[32]   See, e.g., L.-B. Geiger, "Abstraction et séparation d'après saint Thomas," *Revue des sciences philosophiques et théologiques* 31 (1947), 3-40; R. Schmidt, "L'Emploi de la séparation en métaphysique," *Revue philosophique de Louvain* 58 (1960), 376-393; J. Owens, "Metaphysical Separation in Aquinas," *Mediaeval Studies* 34 (1972), 287-306; J. Wippel, "Metaphysics and *Separatio* in Thomas Aquinas," *The Review of Metaphysics* 31 (1978), 431-470.

[33]   E.g., while Corbin's *Le chemin de la théologie chez Thomas d'Aquin* treats the first three questions, it does not really even consider the last three questions, let alone where they would lead. Weisheipl's *Friar Thomas d'Aquino* treats the last two questions, but not the first four, and again gives no indication as to the full intentions of Aquinas.

An Analysis of the Expositio

In Corbin's treatment, he actually begins his analysis with Question 2, because he sees this as the first question properly concerned with the status of theological science and theological methodology.[34] However, he later does include Question 1 in his analysis.[35] Thus, Corbin's approach is not fully consistent here, or at least not clear in its reasoning.

The best place to begin the analysis is even before Question 1, i.e., to begin the analysis with the "Prologue" of Aquinas, not so much to see what is proposed for theological methodology as to see what is practiced. The next logical point to be treated, even before Aquinas' own Question 1, is Aquinas' commentary on the "Preface" of Boethius. All this should be before treating Question 2.

The "Prologue" of Aquinas

The "Prologue" of Aquinas seeks to accomplish several things. The point of departure is the text of Wisdom 6,24: "Ab initio nativitatis investigabo et ponam in lucem scientiam illius" ("I will seek her out from the beginning of her birth, and bring the knowledge of her to light"). Although the Latin term here is "scientiam," the point of Aquinas' "Prologue" is to stress the theme of divine wisdom graciously communicated in revelation, bringing a mysterious "knowledge" of God. The next point of the "Prologue" is to distinguish the theological search for wisdom from the domain of rational metaphysics. The third point of the "Prologue" is to attempt, in a very medieval style, to integrate the text of Wisdom, used as a point of departure, with the structure and purpose of the work of the *De Trinitate* of Boethius, which is the same basic type of approach used by Aquinas in his opening biblical reflection in his *Commentary on the Sentences*.

Aquinas begins with a rhetorical lament:

> Naturalis mentis humanae intuitus pondere corruptibilis corporis aggravatus in prima veritatis luce, ex qua omnia sunt facile cognoscibilia, defigi non potest.[36]

---

[34]   Corbin, *Le chemin de la théologie chez Thomas d'Aquin*, pp. 291-298, esp. p. 299.

[35]   E.g., on p. 323, where he treats q. 1, a. 2, ad 1; and pp. 338-339, where he treats q. 1, a. 2, corpus. But then on p. 348 Corbin continues to refer the Question 2 as if it were the first Question of the work directly concerned with the status of theological science and theological methodology.

[36]   Aquinas, "Prologue," (p. 45). The natural intuition of the human mind, burdened as it is by weight of a corruptible body, is not able to fix its gaze in the first light of truth, in which all things are easily knowable.

Natural reason must advance from posterior, created effects, to the prior, uncreated Cause. But, as Aquinas will often say, with regard to rational metaphysics, it is even difficult to know the ways to proceed, let alone to implement those ways.

> Et ideo deus humano generi aliam tutam viam cognitionis providit, suam notitiam mentibus hominum per fidem infundens.[37]

This is a nuanced statement. "Aliam tutam viam cognitionis" certainly does not speak of demonstrative, scientific knowledge, but of a "way," a "path." Then Aquinas immediately sets up a further tension in his citation of 1 Cor. 2,11: "The things that are of God no man knows, but only the Spirit of God, but to us God has revealed them by his Spirit." So, the tension is between the "way" to knowledge of God that is possible for finite, human beings and the full knowledge of God which only God has of himself.

In this "Prologue," rather than taking an approach to the revelation of God by God's Spirit acting in and through the created order, the experience of the secular world, Aquinas stresses an immediate knowledge of God and even a theological "consideration" of God which, in some unspecified sense, comes "before" the consideration of the created order. And this is exactly the way in which he had begun his *Commentary on the Sentences*:[38]

> Sicut ergo naturalis cognitionis principium est creaturae notitia a sensu accepta, ita cognitionis desuper datae principium est primae veritatis notitia per fidem infusa. Et hinc est quod diverso ordine hinc inde proceditur. Philosophi enim, qui naturalis cognitionis ordinem sequuntur, praeordinant scientiam de creaturis scientiae divinae, scilicet naturalem metaphysicae. Sed apud theologos proceditur e converso, ut creatoris consideratio considerationem praeveniat creaturae.[39]

One thus encounters here again an exceptionally fundamental problem. First of all, there is only a sense in which *the* principle of natural cognition of sensory data is in sensed objects or in the senses. What Aquinas refers to here is a "creaturae notitia," a "notion of created things," as the principle of natural cognition, and this is very close to his meaning and terminology when he

---

[37] Ibid. And for this reason God has provided for humanity another safe way of cognition, giving to the minds of human persons, by means of faith, a notion of himself.

[38] See our "Immediacy and Mediation in Aquinas: 'In I Sent.,' Q. 1, A. 5," *The Thomist* 53 (1989), 31-55.

[39] Aquinas, "Prologue," (pp. 45-46). Therefore, as the principle of natural cognition is the notion of created things, obtained by means of the senses, so too the principle of the cognition of those things which are beyond the natural order is the notion of the first truth, which is infused by means of faith. As a result there is a different order of procedure. Philosophers, who follow the way of natural cognition, order the science of creatures as prior to the science of divine things, that is, metaphysics. But theologians proceed in the reverse order, so that the consideration of the Creator comes prior to the consideration of creatures.

refers to a "notio entis" - which is not abstracted as such.[40] In Aquinas' full epistemological system, the "notio entis" is not the notion of any particular being, and in this sense the "notio entis" is "contentless." The "notio entis" emerges in the human subject because of the level of participated "Esse" which the human subject enjoys, and this enables the human subject to participate in the more "immediate" mode of knowledge of the separate substances and God. However, there is a limitation effecting this participation. The separate substances are able to have immediate knowledge, i.e., knowledge not requiring abstraction of singulars. These substances have immediate knowledge of the created order, themselves, and God. However, the participated "Esse" of the human subject is not intense enough to allow for such immediate knowledge. The "notio entis" and the First Principles of reason (as well as knowledge of the self and of God) cannot be brought to knowledge on a purely a priori basis. Sensory experience is required, but the sensory experience is not adequate as such to account for the "notio entis" and knowledge of the First Principles of reason.

Accordingly Aquinas states here that "the notion of created things" is "obtained *by means of* the senses" [emphasis added], rather than resulting from the senses simply as such. The further point of importance, again, is that the "notio entis" and the First Principles do not contain in themselves the "content" of any particular thing; rather, they apply to things in general.

Now, what Aquinas is doing in this text, as he in fact often does, is to draw an analogy between natural and divine knowledge. The status of the analogical discourse is clearly indicated by the construction "sicut ... ita" ("even as ... so too"). The basic point of the analogy is that even as there is a principle of natural cognition, so too there must be a principle of supernatural cognition, i.e., a "primae veritatis notitia per fidem infusa." Now, if one stresses the similarity in the analogy, the "primae veritatis notitia" is like the "creaturae notitia," at least in the sense that both "notions" serve as principles. But, as has been pointed out, there is also a sense in which the "notio entis" and the First Principles, which are the principles of natural cognition, are more like "infused" knowledge and are "contentless," in that they do not refer to any particular thing but to things in general. In the human subject the "notio entis" and the First Principles are not known until there is the actual abstraction of the form of a material substance, and it is only then, in and through that act of abstraction, that it is realized that a "notio entis" and the First Principles are also known as presupposed. Such knowledge is thus something like "infused" knowledge in that it does not result from abstraction as its sufficient cause.

---

[40] See discussion in our "Lumen Intellectus Agentis: The Participationist-Transcendental Ground of Human Knowledge in the Philosophy of Thomas Aquinas." This sense of "creaturae notitia" is not reflected in Maurer's translation: "knowledge of creatures," and the sense of "suam notitiam" is not reflected in his translation: "his knowledge" (p. 3).

Now, the question which follows is the status of knowledge which can result from the "primae veritatis notitia per fidem infusa." If one stresses the similarities of this to the "notio entis," then one may say that there is a sense in which the "primae veritatis notitia" is "contentless." It is also fitting that it be considered "contentless" because, by definition, this "notion" is of God, who cannot be made into "content" as an "object," strictly speaking. If the analogy to the natural order holds, then the human subject does not have a sufficient a priori knowledge of God, but only the ability to come to knowledge of God through the activity of actually having experience in the world, and engaging in abstraction and reasoning. Furthermore, what Aquinas is talking about here in the supernatural order is "faith." The "primae veritatis notitia" is "per fidem infusa." And thus the broader question here is the status of the act of faith. If the analogy to the natural order holds closely, then the "light of faith" does not result in and of itself in "content," but only arrives at "content" in the very act of being conjoined to a subject who abstracts forms in the sensible world, i.e., a subject engaged in experience.

By an extension of the discussion one may note that the articles of faith are "entities" in human language; they are sensible enunciations in the created order. The articles of faith are not known on an a priori basis, either as a result of the natural "light" of the intellect or as an a priori result of the "infused light" of faith. The articles of faith can be "known" only upon an experience of them as sensible entities in language - "faith comes upon hearing." It is the material of the articles of faith that then provides the material for the act of assent in faith, even though faith is not ultimately directed to the articles as its end, but to the First Truth Itself. Because the articles of faith can be known only after experience, one may say that the "light of faith" itself is "contentless" and experience provides the "material content" of faith. What faith can be said to provide is an "instinct for God," an interpretive principle of discernment for what is to be assented to in finite discourse as a moment in the movement to the First Truth.

In the above text of Aquinas, and in many others, his tendency is to stress the "primae veritatis notitia per fidem infusa," or the "lumen fidei," as providing the actual "material" for the assent of faith. This could be at least a consistent theological position if Aquinas were completely devoted to a Platonic or Neoplatonic epistemology. But he is not. His whole epistemology of knowledge of the First Principles is directly Aristotelian, i.e., based on the structure of the agent intellect and the necessity of the abstraction of the forms of material substances. The problem in the above text is that it can at least be read and understood as meaning that there is some sort of possible "theological" knowledge which completely circumvents the "natural" order of cognition. This problem comes to the surface in the above text when Aquinas states that in contrast to the procedure of natural cognition, the theologian considers the Creator prior to the consideration of creatures. The obvious problem here is the same one that can be found in other texts of Aquinas: it is difficult - if not impossible - to provide any sort of meaningful explanation as to how the theologian could obtain absolutely immediate knowledge of God, i.e., absolutely prior to knowledge of the created order. It seems more feasible to say that knowledge of God is obtained through the created order and faith then structures the interpretation of the created order, and structures the intentional priority of the consideration of God in theology; but God is never directly considered, In- and Of-Himself, Per Se. Indeed, this is the very structure which Aquinas actually follows in his own *Expositio* of Boethius in the questions which follow. Aquinas does not immediately begin with God, but with a reflection on the created order, in this case, the processes of human cognition. The only way Aquinas could practice such immediate theology would have to include the absence of theological texts, and the absence of any language or discursive thought. But such silence is not possible in a theological text.

Aquinas then considers, in more Aristotelian fashion, the "materia, modus et finis" ("the matter, the mode, and the end") of Boethius' *De Trinitate*. It is here, in Aquinas' comments about the "matter" of the *De Trinitate*, that Aquinas reveals his consideration of the theological tractates of Boethius as forming an integrated whole.[41] The significant thing here is that Aquinas reveals his sense of the unity of the Boethian theological tractates. There is a certain teaching of the faith concerning the Trinity, which by tradition speaks of a Trinity of Persons, Father, Son, and Holy Spirit. But to theologically consider this mystery of revelation means also to inquire into the meaningfulness of finite, analogical predication concerning God. A partial meaningfulness is recovered by means of the theory of participation which Boethius reflects in his *De Hebdomadibus*. The salvific reparation of humanity in a Trinitarian dynamism will particularly integrate christology, Trinitarian theology, and grace, in the attempt to consider the incarnation as uniting a human nature with a divine Person. The task is indeed broad and difficult, but Aquinas indicates here his sense of the themes involved in a comprehensive Trinitarian theology attempting to treat the core thematic of Christian faith.

There then follows another dialectical shift in the comments of Aquinas. The structure and the contents are almost exactly like the shift in the *Commentary on the Sentences*. Only shortly before in this "Prologue," Aquinas has stated that there is a knowledge of the first truth which is infused by faith, and that the theologian considers the Creator before considering creatures. But at the end of this "Prologue" it appears that the knowledge of the first truth which is by means of faith is also by means of acceptance of the teachings of human authorities, e.g., the "fathers" of the Church. Here the

---

[41] See, again, Aquinas, "Prologue," (pp. 46-47), cited above.

stress is more on faith both as contained in the preached message and a response to the preached message. But in either case there is a finite mediation and a sense in which the faithed-hearer's intentionality is ordered toward the finite symbols of the preached Gospel. Just how the theologian could have such an a priori consideration of the Creator and then consider creatures is not clarified here by Aquinas. The only distinction made at the end of the "Prologue" is that the Trinity may be considered or investigated by means of the teachings of the authorities, but this is certainly *not* a purely a priori consideration by means of the "immediate light" of divine revelation! Aquinas also states here that some investigation of the Trinity is possible by means of reason (meaning not that reason can discover the mystery of the Trinity, but that after acceptance of the mystery in faith, there can be a search undertaken by reason for some partial understanding). But this is, again, *not* a purely a priori investigation. The dialectical point here is that whether one considers the Trinity via the "authorities" or via "reason" or both, there is mediation rather than immediate "content" by way of "the divine light of inspiration."And when one says that theology can investigate the Trinity in some way by means of reason, this means that such a theology is obviously not constituted prior to an engagement with natural knowledge.[42]

The theologian is not accorded any sort of absolutely immediate knowledge of God or of the truths of the faith as such. All such knowledge is mediated, and the stress is on the mediation of the teaching and preaching of the "fathers" of the church. But there is a further movement which Aquinas literally regards as a "manifestation" of the truths of the faith, a movement in which reason, while guided by the intentionality of faith and presupposing the truths of faith, seeks to transverse its own proper domain, in a process which transforms reason into something which could more accurately, yet still vaguely, be specified as "dialectical, mystical wisdom."

The Commentary of Aquinas on the "Preface" of Boethius

The "Preface" of Boethius is itself rich in thought. His initial statement utilizes a complex, Neoplatonic analogy.[43] With this analogy, Boethius is assigning a principal agency to the divinity regarding his own process of

---

[42] See, again, Aquinas, "Prologue," (pp. 47-48), cited above.

[43] Boethius, Tractate I, *De Trinitate* (p. 2): "Investigatam diutissime quaestionem, quantum nostrae mentis igniculum lux divina dignata est, formatam rationibus litterisque mandatam offerendam vobis communicandamque curavi tam vestri cupidus iudicii quam nostri studiosus inventi."

"I have very long pondered this question, so far as the divine light has deemed it fitting to enkindle the feeble spark of my mind. Now, having set it forth in logical order and cast it into literary form, I have caused it to be presented and communicated to you, being as much desirous of your judgement as zealous for my own discovery."

theological reflection. The basis for this "illuminationist" analogy in Boethius would seem to be Augustine, whom Boethius immediately acknowledges in this "Preface."[44]

In Aquinas' commentary on the "Preface" of Boethius he does some expected and, perhaps, some profound and unexpected things. Given Aquinas' fondness for Aristotelian analysis, he interprets the "Preface" of Boethius as indicating the "four causes" of the work: the material cause (the subject matter to be investigated), the (secondary) efficient cause (the "feeble spark" of the mind of Boethius), the principal efficient cause as such (the "divine light"), the formal cause (the logical organization of the work), and the final cause (as the manifestation of hidden, mysterious truth not for the many, but for the wise). The basic manner of Aristotelian division here is expected. But some profound an unclarified distinctions are made with regard to the efficient causes of the theological activity of Boethius, and, by implication, of Aquinas himself:

> Secundo tangit causam efficientem: et proximam sive secundariam in hoc quod dicit: 'quantum mentis nostrae igniculum,' et primam sive principalem in hoc quod dicit: 'illustrare lux divina dignata est.' Proxima siquidem causa huius investigationis fuit intellectus auctoris, qui recte igniculus dicitur. Ignis enim, ut dicit Dionysius 15 c. *Caelestis hierarchiae,* maxime competit ad significandas divinas proprietates, tum ratione subtilitatis, tum ratione luminis, tum ratione virtutis activae per calorem, tum ratione situs et motus. Quae quidem deo maxime competunt, in quo est summa simplicitas et immaterialitas, perfecta claritas, omnipotens virtus et altissima sublimitas, angelis autem mediocriter, sed humanis mentibus infimo modo, quarum propter corpus coniunctum et puritas inquinatur et lux obscuratur et virtus debilitatur et motus in suprema retardatur; unde humanae mentis efficacia recte igniculo comparatur. Unde nec ad huius quaestionis veritatem inquirendam sufficit, nisi divina luce illustrata, et sic divina lux est causa principalis, humana mens causa secondaria.[45]

---

[44] Ibid. (p. 4): "Ad quantum haec difficilior quaestio est, tam facilior esse debet ad veniam. Vobis tamen etiam illud inspiciendum est, an ex beati Augustini scriptis semina rationum aliquos in nos venientia fructus extulerint."

"In proportion to the difficulty of a problem, the pardoning of error ought to be more easily granted. You, however, determine whether the 'semina rationum' sown in my mind by St. Augustine's writings have borne fruit."

[45] Aquinas, *Expositio Super Librum Boethii De Trinitate* (p. 50). Secondly, he indicates the efficient cause, proximate or secondary, when he says, 'the feeble spark of my mind.' And he speaks of the principal or first cause when he says, 'which the divine light has enkindled.' The proximate cause of this investigation is the intellect of the author, which is rightly termed a spark. For fire, as Dionysius says in Chapter 15 of the *Caelestial Hierarchy,* maximally pertains to signifying divine properties, by reason of its subtlety, its light, its active power by means of heating, and also its place and motion. These things pertain to God in the highest degree, for in God is the summit of simplicity and immateriality, perfect clarity, omnipotent power and the highest sublimity. To the angels, however, 'fire' pertains to a lesser degree, and to human minds in an even weaker mode, for on account of their unions with bodies, their purity is reduced, their

The importance of this text, and the problems raised by it, can hardly be overestimated. The investigation of the status and method of theology brings one immediately to the problematic of real and free human secondary causality in the philosophy and theology of Aquinas. One must recall here the formulation of the more youthful Aquinas, when in Question 1, Article 1 of the *Commentary on the Sentences* he would state that the "divine light of inspiration" *is* "theology." In that earlier formulation, there is no suggestion of secondary causality in Article 1, but the dialectical tensions in Article 5 do suggest something like secondary causality.

The exact meaning of "secondary causality" is very hard to penetrate.[46] The technical term, "secondary causality," may at first sound like precise conceptual discourse, but in reality it is more of a limit-concept, because the full referential meaning of it cannot be grasped, even on a philosophical level.

The next important thing to be noted here is that Aquinas is actually following Boethius in using a double analogy in an *ex convenientia* mode of discourse. Referring to the human intellect as a "spark" is an analogy, and the extension of this analogy to God as a more powerful and fully actualized "divine light" is extending what is already a metaphor, and so its referential value can only be quite limited. The next thing to be noted is that there is an apparent contradiction, or at least a serious tension, in Aquinas' description of the effects of the body on this human, intellectual "spark." The contradiction, or tension, is that Aquinas here takes a very Platonic stance, as if the human mind would be able to know more accurately and fully without sense knowledge - as if the "light," or being, of the human intellect were capable of knowing essences in themselves but is unfortunately tied down to a body. Now, if Aquinas uses the metaphor of "spark" to refer to the level of "esse" of the human subject, which is the only more specific meaning that makes more consistent sense in the broader context of his epistemology and metaphysics, then he would be saying that the level of "esse" of which the human form is capable is limited and held back by the body, as the "matter" informed by that form. But this seems to go against Aquinas' often stated principle that the level of "esse" is determined simply by the form, as an active principle communicating "esse," while matter is a passive principle receiving "esse." The above text has matter, rather than form, limiting "esse." But a substantial change in "esse" can only be accounted for by a substantial change in form.

---

light is obscured, their power weakened, and their upward motion retarded. Hence the efficacy of the human mind is rightly compared to a spark. Thus this spark does not suffice for this inquiry into the truth, unless it is illuminated [enkindled] by divine light, and this divine light is the principal cause, while the human mind is a secondary cause.

[46] See discussion in B. Lonergan, "On God and Secondary Causes," *Collection: Papers by Bernard Lonergan*, ed. F. Crowe (New York: Herder and Herder, 1968).

An underlying problem here is Aquinas' view of the "separability" of the human form. As is reflected in his later "Treatise on Man," in the *Summa Theologiae*, Aquinas distinguished three basic types of forms: those that could exist only in matter, such as the lower forms of inanimate objects; those that could exist only independently of matter, such as the forms of the separate substances and The Form of God; and those forms that could exist either in matter or independently of matter, namely, those of human beings.[47] The motivating factor for Aquinas' treatment of the human form as "separable" certainly included his theological view of death, immortality, and resurrection. If the human form continues to exist after death but "prior" to resurrection, then this form must be "separable." Of course, Aquinas could not demonstrate that this particular viewpoint had to be the case, since it involves a theological presupposition.

What results from all of this is a particular tension in the formulations of Aquinas regarding the status of the human form. Normally, "esse" is limited simply by form, as form is the first act of a substance, which contains in itself its own principle of limitation of "esse." Form is regarded as "active" with respect to the "passivity" of "matter," as mere potentiality. "Matter," as potentiality, limits the type of form which can be received, but it is, properly speaking, the type of form that limits the level of "esse." The particular tension in Aquinas' formulations about the human form is that he holds that it is capable of existing without matter, in a completely "immaterial" condition (meaning "immaterial" in all senses of "materialilty"), and yet in this life this form exists only with matter, and after the resurrection it exists with a type of "matter," although such "matter" would be radically different in "nature." Aquinas actually argues in "The Treatise on Man" for the fittingness of "corporeal resurrection," because the human form is not suited to existence separate from matter. Such an existence without matter would be "against the nature" of the human form, and in the "Treatise on Man" in the *Summa Theologiae* I, Aquinas argues that in such a state of existence, separated from matter, the human soul would be able to have only a confused knowledge. In that Treatise Aquinas attempted to avoid the tension that would have resulted if he had argued for a relief from this confused knowledge by means of directly inflused knowledge from God - and this *prior* to resurrection - since this would have made the state of the soul prior to resurrection too much like the state of the soul after resurrection and Beatific Vision. Thus Aquinas argued that the human soul separated from matter can have only a confused knowledge. But the fact remains that in that Treatise Aquinas argues not that the body retards the soul, but that the body perfects the operations of the soul, and is even needed in Beatific Vision, precisely because of the nature of the

---

[47]   The "forms" of the celestial bodies are distinct, complicating cases which do not need to be considered for present purposes, let alone the question of their type of matter.

human form. Thus, relative to that position, Aquinas' formulation here in the *Expositio* of the *De Trinitate* is more blatantly Neoplatonic, for he is not arguing here for the appropriateness of a new type of matter for the human form, but simply that the present corporeal condition of human existence reduces the purity of the mind and obscures intellectual light, which is said to be more of a "spark," a type of potentiality, than actualized "fire." Be this as it may, the strained impression given in the text as it stands is that if the human form were simply liberated from corporeal existence, its intellectual light would not be so reduced, but actually expanded. In the "Treatise on Man," Aquinas does not argue this, but almost the opposite.

The next problem that should be noted is the difficult interplay of the two metaphors. The human intellect is referred to as a "spark" while the divine is more properly said to be a "fire." Some discussion of this problem has already been provided above concerning the text of Boethius himself. Basically following Boethius, Aquinas states that the "spark" of the human mind is "illuminated by divine light" ("divina luce illustrata"). Again, as in the time of Boethius, Aquinas would have equated "light" with "fire," and the difficulty in the metaphors is the extent to which one would understand the "illumination" to entail an identity of essence between the divine light (fire) which "illumines" and the feeble "spark" which is "illuminated." If this "illumination" is by direct contact, so that the very flames of the larger fire are communicated to weak sparks, then there is an resulting identity of essence between the source and the recipient. But if the stronger fire "illuminates" the weak sparks from a distance, then there is not a resulting identity of essence. Perhaps the straining of language - or at least of conceptual understanding - is necessary here.

Aquinas would not want to give the impression of univocity by saying that the "spark" of the human intellect is given the very "fire" of the divine substance. Nevertheless it is a strained interplay of metaphors, hardly possible to imagine in any concrete, analogical sense. In the natural order, if there were remnant embers still containing weak sparks, and these weak sparks could be seen as faintly glowing in the night, and then a large, radiantly burning fire were brought within close proximity of those sparks, there is a sense in which the weak sparks could be "illuminated" by the more powerful light from the stronger fire. But it is a strange kind of "illumination" in that, in such a case, the faint glimmerings of the weak sparks would be "seen" to disappear in the brighter light of the proximate fire. In the more normal sense of "illumination" one would have something like the case of a morning sunrise illuminating the mountain peaks on the horizon, which could not be seen in the darkness of the night. Such an illumination makes the object appear. The phrasing of Aquinas is in a way more problematic, for if a "weak spark" is "illuminated" by a more powerful light, at least in the natural order, what is communicated is not an "enkindling," but an illumination that seems to make the light of the weak spark disappear rather than increase. The fundamental point here is that the conceptual meaning of the double analogy is very hard to penetrate. Even if one does away with the problem of "spark" and "light" and simply refers to the human intellect as a "weak light" and God as "absolute light," Aquinas is still engaged in the realm of metaphor and is not saying what this further illumination could involve or exactly how it occurs. To shift from the metaphor of "light" to the more precise, metaphysical language of "being" does not enable a solution to the problem either. For if the substantial "being," "esse," of a subject is increased, then the subject has changed into another substance. The only intelligible meaning, still hard to penetrate, is that there can be an type of increase in the "accidental" "being" of the subject, by means of a more intense participation in Being Itself, which affects the intentional horizon of the subject, but does not transform substantial being.

Perhaps the very difficult and unarticulated "solution" here is what it means for God to be the principal cause of all theological activity, and, indeed, of all human activity, and all the activity of the universe, and still allow for real secondary causality. To limit the discussion somewhat to theology, there seems to be a sense in which all the activity of the theologian pre-exists in God, and one is left with a sort of Plotinian dualism, in which the activity of the theologian as caused principally and known most fully by God himself is more "real" than the secondary and caused activity of the theologian himself or herself. This is actually the point of both Boethius and Aquinas.

Question 1: Human Knowledge of Divine Things

Question 1 is, indeed, a valuable question, even though not directly analyzed by Corbin. This Question consists of four articles: 1) whether the human mind needs an additional illumination by divine light in order to know the truth, 2) whether the human mind is able to know God, 3) whether God is the first thing known by the human mind, and 4) whether natural reason suffices for human knowledge of the divine Trinity.

Article 1: Additional Illumination

Here the concern is with the status of the created, human intellect, and whether an additional illumination is needed, over and above that granted the agent intellect in the very act of creation, in order for the human intellect to come to knowledge of any truth whatsoever. The Article is concerned, therefore, with the participated status of the agent intellect. One can see here that Aquinas is beginning his treatment with participationist thematics, which were particularly on his mind at this time, during which he also wrote his *Commentary on the De Hebdomadibus.* Already in the *Sed contra* Aquinas states what will be his classic position; and while a *Sed contra* cannot be taken as Aquinas' own answer to the problem, it does at least give an indication as to what Aquinas saw as involved in the problem.

> Sed contra, mens humana illustrata est divinitus lumine naturali, secundum illud Psalmi (4,7): 'Signatum est super nos lumen vultus tui, domine.' Si ergo hoc lumen, quia creatum est, non sufficit ad veritatem conspiciendam, sed requirit novam illustrationem, pari ratione lumen superadditum non sufficiet, sed indigebit alio lumine, et sic in infinitum, quod numquam compleri potest, et sic impossibile erit cognoscere aliquam veritatem. Ergo oportet stare in primo lumine, ut scilicet mens lumine naturali sine aliquo superaddito possit veritatem videre.[48]

In the body of the Article, Aquinas attempts to further clarify the status of the participated light of the human intellect as an active potentiality:

> Responsio. Dicendum quod haec est differentia inter virtutes activas et passivas quod passivae non possunt exire in actum propriae operationis, nisi moveantur a suis activis, sicut sensus non sentit, nisi moveatur a sensibili, sed virtutes activae possunt operari sine hoc quod ab alio moveantur, sicut patet in viribus animae vegetabilis.
>
> Sed in genere intellectus invenitur duplex potentia: activa, scilicet intellectus agens, et passiva, scilicet intellectus possibilis. Quidam vero posuerunt quod solus intellectus possibilis erat potentia animae, intellectus vero agens erat quaedam substantia separata. Et haec est opinio Avicennae … . Sed quia verba Philosophi in III De anima magis videntur sonare quod intellectus agens sit potentia animae et huic etiam auctoritas sacrae scripturae consonat, quae lumine intelligibili nos insignitos esse profitetur, cui Philosophus comparat intellectum agentem, ideo in anima ponitur respectu intelligibilis operationis, quae est cognitio veritatis, et potentia passiva et potentia activa.[49]

---

[48]   Aquinas, *Expositio Super Librum Boethii De Trinitate*, q. 1, a. 1, sc (pp. 58-59). On the contrary, the human mind is divinely illuminated by its natural light, according to the saying of the Psalm [4,7]: 'The light of your countenance, O Lord, is signed upon us.' If, therefore, this light, which is created, is not sufficient for the knowledge of the truth, but requires a new illumination, this superadded light would not suffice either, but would require still another light, and so on into infinity, which in no way can be encompassed, and thus it would be impossible to know any sort of truth. Therefore it follows that the human mind must stand in the first light, namely, that the human mind by means of its natural light and without the further addition of any other light, is able to see the truth.

[49]   Ibid., q. 1, a. 1, resp. (pp. 59-60). I respond, it is to be said that there is a difference between active powers and passive powers in that passive powers are not able to move into their own proper operation unless moved to do so by their active agents, even as a sense does not sense unless moved by a sensible object. But active powers are capable of operating without being moved by another, as is clear in the powers of the vegetative soul.

However, this active power of the agent intellect is a created and finite power. It does have a sufficient participation in divine Light to grasp the first principles of reason, but it does not have a sufficient participation in divine Light to grasp those things which exceed the realm of human reason, and for any knowledge of such things it will be necessary for the human subject to receive an additional illumination, over and above that granted the human subject simply in virtue of creation.

Thus already in this first Article Aquinas is concerned with the relationship between the light of natural reason and the light of faith. In the response to the fourth objection, Aquinas further qualifies the status of this natural light as mediated in the human subject by the corporeal existence of the human subject in this life, and this can hamper or limit the extent to which the powers of this natural light are actually put into operation:

> Ad quartum dicendum quod lumen intelligibile, ubi est purum sicut in angelis, sine difficultate omnia cognita naturaliter demonstrat, ita quod in eis est omnia naturalia cognoscere. In nobis autem lumen intelligibile est obumbratum per coniunctionem ad corpus et ad vires corporeas, et ex hoc impeditur, ut non libere possit veritatem etiam naturaliter cognoscibilem inspicere, secundum illud Sap. 10 (9,15): 'Corpus quod corrumpitur' etc. Et exinde est quod non est omnino in nobis veritatem cognoscere, scilicet propter impedimenta. Sed unusquisque magis vel minus habet hoc in potestate, secundum quod lumen intelligibile est in ipso purius.[50]

A fundamental problem here is that Aquinas does not specify how this intelligible light can become more "pure" in a person. He does imply that this process of purification has something to do with a release from the burden

---

But in the case of intellectual things, a twofold potentiality is found: an active potentiality, namely, the agent intellect, and a passive potentiality, namely, the possible intellect. Now there are those who have considered that only the possible intellect is a potentiality of the soul, while the agent intellect is some sort of separate substance. And this is the opinion of Avicenna [*De Anima* V, c. 5] ... . But because the words of the Philosopher in III *De Anima* seem to proclaim more convincingly that the active intellect is a potency of the soul, and because with this the authority of Sacred Scripture agrees [Cf. Ps. 4,7: "The light of your countenance"], which declares that we are distinguished by the intellectual light which is signed upon us, which the Philosopher compares to the agent intellect, for the same reason it is thought that there is in the soul with respect to intelligible operation, which is knowledge of the truth, both a passive potency and an active potency.

[50] Ibid., q. 1, a. 1, ad 4 (p. 62). To the fourth objection it is to be said that intelligible light, where it is pure, as in the angels, naturally demonstrates without difficulty, all things it knows, so that in them there is [the power] to know all natural things [immediately]. In us, however, this intelligible light is obscure, being weighed down by its conjunction with the body and with corporeal powers, and on this account it is hindered and it is not able to freely behold that truth which is naturally knowable, as is said in Wisdom 10 [9,15]: 'For the corruptible body,' etc. ["is a load upon the soul; and this earthly habitation burdens down the thoughtful mind"]. From this it follows that on account of the impediment [of the body], we do not know all truth. But each one possesses more or less the power [to know the truth] according to the purity of intelligible light which is in him.

which the corruptible body places upon the soul; but he does not clarify here how there can be differences in the degree of intelligible light among various people, and he does not resolve the problematic, in comparison with "The Treatise on Man" in the *Summa Theologiae*, that without a body the human soul is actually in a more inferior state, not in accord with its nature, than it has when it is united with a body. What is also lacking here in this text is a clarification of the relationship of intelligible light in angels and in human beings. As the text stands it can give the impression that the intellectual light possessed by angels and human beings is essentially the same type of thing, and it is only on account of the corporeal existence of human beings that this intellectual light is hindered. But this simply exaggerates the "angelic nature" of human beings. It would be more accurate, in Aquinas' line of thought, to say that their levels of being, "esse," differ, and thus the levels of intrinsic intelligibility of the intellectual light possessed by angels and human beings differ, with this difference allowing angelic intellects to know essences immediately, without abstraction, while requiring such abstraction on the part of the human intellect.

One should recall here that the point of Article 1 is whether an additional illumination is needed in order for the human intellect to come to any knowledge of the truth. In the fourth objection it was stated that the human subject does not have the power to know truth, because it is evident that many labor in order to arrive at the truth but do not attain it. The objection was that it is thus evident that the human subject does not have a sufficient internal principle, of intellectual light, for coming to know the truth and thus an additional illumination is necessary. The contextual point of Aquinas' reply is simply that human beings possess intellectual light to varying degrees, and thus it is possible for some to labor without attaining the truth, while others may attain the truth. Nevertheless, Aquinas' additional argumentation in the reply can give the false impression that the distinction between the angelic and the human intellect is simply the corporeal condition of human being.

In the reply to the seventh objection, there is a further observation of particular interest:

Ad septimum dicendum quod voluntas numquam potest bene velle sine divino instincto, potest autem bene velle sine gratiae infusione, sed non meritorie. Et similiter intellectus non potest sine divino motu veritatem quamcumque cognoscere, potest autem sine novi luminis infusione, quamvis non ea quae naturalem cognitionem excedunt.[51]

---

[51]   Ibid., q. 1, a. 1, ad 7 (p. 63). To the seventh objection it is to be said that the will is never able to will the good without a divine instinct, however it is able to will the good without infused grace, but non-meritoriously. And similarly the intellect is not able to know any truth whatsoever without [an initiating] divine motion, however it is able to know [truth, some truth] without a new infusion of light, although not those [truths] which exceed natural cognition.

Here the initial objection concerns the position that "voluntas non potest bene velle nisi divina gratia adiuvetur," a position which Aquinas cites from Augustine in order to draw a parallel objection concerning the intellect. Objection 7 states:

> Praeterea, sicut se habet voluntas ad bene volendum, ita se habet intellectus ad recte intelligendum. Sed voluntas non potest bene velle, nisi divina gratia adiuvetur, ut Augustinus dicit. Ergo nec intellectus potest veritatem intelligere, nisi divina luce illustretur.[52]

If the will is unable to will the good in an effective manner without the aid of divine grace, it could also seem that the intellect is unable to know any truth without an additional illumination of grace. The reply of Aquinas is making a distinction: the human will can will the good that is natural to it by the power given to it merely in virtue of creation, but this willing of a natural good is not meritorious in the order of grace. The reply of Aquinas is problematic here, even as the context of Augustine's arguments against Pelagianism was problematic. Augustine had to stress that in order for the human subject to know, will, and do the good on the salvific level, grace was absolutely necessary, and this in part because of the effects of original sin. But this does not mean that there is a pure nature of the human subject in a "fallen state" which is totally independent and distinct from the order of grace. It is certainly not the position of Aquinas that the orders of nature and grace, or reason and faith, are independent and separate; rather, grace perfects nature. Even as there is an ordering of the will, given simply in virtue of creation, to its ultimate end of beatitude in loving possession of God, so too there is an ordering of the intellect, given simply in virtue of creation, to its ultimate end of beatitude in intentional unity with God. In the broader context of Aquinas' theology, it is not the case that there is a "natural will" unaffected by grace, and it is not the case that there is a "natural intellect" unaffected by grace. It is the case that grace admits of different levels of participation.[53] It is the case, as Aquinas clearly states here, that the human subject is able to come to knowledge of the truth, simply through the natural light of reason, but such knowledge can only be of that which is within its own natural range. The exact way in which the will can will well without divine assistance is not clarified here, nor is the distinction between natural knowledge of the truth and knowledge of supernatural truth.

---

[52] Ibid., ob 7 (p. 58). Further, as the will is related to willing well, so is the intellect related to right understanding. But the will cannot will well unless it is aided by grace, as Augustine says [*Contra duas Epistulas Pelagianorum* I, c. 3, n. 7]. Therefore neither is the intellect able to understand the truth, unless it is illuminated by divine light.

[53] One enters here into a classical debate, points of which are still voiced by A. Vergote and J. Walgrave, concerning "desire" for God.

Article 2: Human Knowledge of God

There are many types of human knowledge. The human subject is capable of arriving at knowledge that is not simply the result of a process of the abstraction of "form," but of a metaphysical process of reasoning, ultimately involving negation in the judgement of *separatio*, as Aquinas will make clear in Questions 5 and 6 of this very work. However, such metaphysical knowledge involves an arduous process, and, for a variety of reasons, mosthuman beings do not reach an explicit and reflective level of such knowledge. The most common and proper process of human knowledge involves the abstraction of a form from a material existent. But this will obviously not suffice for knowledge of God. Another type of human knowledge involves the similarity between a cause and its effect(s), and one can reason from the observed effect(s) to something similar, or analogical, in the cause.

The "form" of God cannot be abstracted by the human subject because the Form of God does not exist in matter and because this "form" as Infinite Act infinitely exceeds the capabilities of finite intellect. In the body of this Article, Aquinas makes an interesting observation in this regard: "non potest ipsum deum cognoscetur in hoc statu per formam quae est essentia sua, sed sic cognoscetur in patria a beatis."[54] One encounters here a limit-point in Aquinas' theological language that is problematic, and which will often appear. The problem here is the level of Aquinas' language. There is a kerygmatic language which announces that in the beatitude of heaven, the human person will see God, "face to face," "as He is." There is also a dogmatic language which uses the metaphysical notions of "form" and "essence" to announce in a kind of dogmatic kerygma that in the beatitude of heaven, the human person will "know God by God's own essence" or that the infinite "form of God will itself be that which is received by the human intellect." In more careful language, one must stress that there is never anything predicated univocally of God and finite creatures, and thus one must say that the Essence and the Form of God is completely known only by God. When Aquinas talks about the beatific vision, he does not always make explicit what level of language he is using.

Theological method is something prior to Beatific Vision, but Aquinas has a teleological tendency to "read backwards" from what the nature of Beatific Vision could be to what the nature of theological reflection should be in this life. The result can be an exaggerated "angelicism" as to how human

---

[54] Aquinas, *Expositio Super Librum Boethii De Trinitate*, q. 1, a. 2, resp. (p. 65). [Our intellect] is not able to know God in this life by means of his form, which is his very essence, but this is the way God is known in heaven by those in beatitude.

understanding, even when enlightened by faith, can come to some "knowledge" of the Trinity.

Question 1, Article 2 is concerned with whether it is possible for the human mind to come to any knowledge of God. There is a "limit-case" of such knowledge in the instance of those, who in some way, enjoy beatitude in heaven. In the response, Aquinas also considers the type of rational knowledge of God that can be attained in metaphysics, which is fundamentally a reasoning from created effects to an analogical knowledge of the Cause. Here Aquinas notes:

> Effectus autem est duplex: quidam, qui adaequatur virtuti suae causae, et per talem effectum cognoscitur plenarie virtus causae, et per consequens quiditas ipsius; alius effectus est, qui deficit a praedicta aequalitate, et per talem effectum non potest comprehendi virtus agentis et per consequens nec essentia eius; sed cognoscitur tantum de causa quod est. Et sic se habet cognitio effectus ut principium ad cognoscendum de causa an est, sicut se habet quiditas ipsius causae, cum per suam formam cognoscitur. Hoc autem modo se habet omnis effectus ad deum. Et ideo non possumus in statu viae pertingere ad cognoscendum de ipso nisi quia est. Et tamen unus cognoscentium quia est alio perfectius cognoscit, quia causa tanto ex effectu perfectius cognoscitur, quanto per effectum magis apprehenditur habitudo causae ad effectum.[55]

Now in this text, Aquinas is discussing a philosophical and metaphysical knowledge of God. The limitations here are quite clear: such means of knowing can only reach a knowledge of God, *quod est*, that God "exists"; with such means of knowing it is not possible to reach knowledge of the *quid est*, or the Essence of God. But there are some very difficult problems here when one considers the broader aspects of systematic consistency in Aquinas' treatment of the relationships of revelation, grace, and Beatific Vision. Aquinas argues that in Beatific Vision there is something of a mediating divine light, the light of glory, which is not God himself but a created entity, and thus an effect of God; but he then argues that this divine light of glory

---

[55]   Ibid., q. 1, a. 2, resp. (pp. 65-66). Effects, however, are of two types: one which adequates [i.e., fully manifests] the power of its cause, and through such an effect the power of its cause is fully known, and consequently the essence of the cause; and there is another type of effect, which is not adequate to the power of its cause, and through this type of effect it is not possible to comprehend the power of the agent and consequently the essence of the agent cannot be comprehended either, but it is only known concerning the cause that it is [*quod est*]. Thus the knowledge of an effect stands as a principle of the knowledge of whether the cause exists [*an est*], even as the essence of the cause itself [serves as a principle of the knowledge of the cause] when the cause is known [essentially] through its own form. It is, however, according to this second mode that every effect stands in relation to God. And for the same reason it is not possible in this life to attain knowledge of God himself [the essence of God], but only that God exists. Nevertheless, among those knowing that God exists, the knowledge of one is more perfect than that of another, because a cause is more perfectly known from its effect to the degree that the relation of the cause to the effect is more fully apprehended.

will proportion the creature for some mysterious knowledge of the Essence of God. One then enters again into limit-discourse, for here one has a created effect somehow communicating the Essence of God - or making such communication possible.

In the response, Aquinas then moves to the realm of theology:

> In hoc autem profectu cognitionis maxime iuvatur mens humana, cum lumen eius naturale nova illustratione confortatur; sicut est lumen fidei et doni sapientiae et intellectus, per quod mens in contemplatione supra se elevari dicitur, in quantum cognoscit deum esse supra omne id, quod naturaliter comprehendit. Sed quia ad eius essentiam videndam penetrare non sufficit, dicitur in se ipsam quodammodo ab excellenti lumine reflecti, et hoc est quod dicitur Gen. 32 (30) super illud: 'Vidi dominum facie ad faciem,' in Glossa Gregorii 'Visus animae, cum in deum intenditur, immensitatis coruscatione reverberatur.'[56]

The first point to note here is that Aquinas is still defending a natural knowledge of God, but only on the level of a knowledge *an sit*. The next thing to note is that Aquinas is referring to the light of faith and to the gifts of wisdom and understanding as providing a "new illumination" of the human mind. This new illumination is not God himself, but in some unspecified way an increased "participation" in God, which raises the mind "above itself" in contemplation of God. There is a dialectic in this contemplation. Aquinas is talking about contemplation of God in this life, aided by a supernatural light. The dialectic is that even with this supernatural light there is no conceptual "content" of God that can be grasped. Even in this contemplation there is a return to the domain of natural human conceptuality, but only for a negation of that conceptuality as adequate to attain the Essence of God himself, which Essence is absolutely beyond the natural domain of human conceptuality. The final point of great importance to note here is that Aquinas then introduces a rather phenomenological analysis of human consciousness as it struggles to reach some understanding of God: God is not attained as an object, but as a "subject" within human intentionality, in the mysterious manner in which the human intellect turns to itself, to see reflected in itself something of the divine Light in its own intentional operations. Even here, this immanent reflection remains a mystery, as the ultimate cause cannot be essentially

---

[56]   Ibid., q. 1, a. 2, resp. (pp. 66-67). In [the attempt to arrive at some knowledge of God] the human mind is maximally assisted when its natural light is fortified by a new illumination, such as the light of faith and the gifts of wisdom and understanding, by which the mind is elevated above itself in contemplation, inasmuch as it knows God to be above anything which it naturally comprehends. But because even this new light does not suffice to penetrate to a vision of his essence, it is said to be, in a certain way, reflected back upon itself by the superior light [i.e., of faith and the gifts of understanding and wisdom]; and this is what is said regarding Genesis 32 [30], 'I Have seen God face to face,' in the gloss of Gregory [cf. *M. Moral.*, XXIV, c. 6, n. 12]: 'When the vision of the soul is directed to God, it is reflected back upon itself, overwhelmed by the brilliance of his immensity.'

grasped, and even in this infused contemplation there is an awareness of the blinding immensity of God as "Other," who cannot be viewed directly. Aquinas is hinting here at such a phenomenology of consciousness, though he does not here, or elsewhere, develop this theme in a fully explicit manner.

In the present response Aquinas is making a distinction between philosophical knowledge of God, and what can be theologically said about other types of knowledge of God. Here Aquinas is doing theology, but he does not mention theology or science: he simply mentions that the natural light of reason can be aided to the greatest extent when strengthened by the new illumination of the light of faith and the gifts of wisdom and understanding. Aquinas does not mention at all the "science of theology"; he does mention that which is presupposed, the light of faith, and two perfections which are, in a way, more profound than the "science of theology," namely, the gifts of wisdom and understanding. What is also important to note here is that Aquinas does not say that with this strengthening light of faith, or with these further gifts - much less with the science of theology - God comes to be known essentially. All Aquinas says here is that even with this additional light and these additional gifts the human mind "knows" God to be above all the things that the human mind can naturally comprehend. It should be well noted here that this remains an indirect manner of "knowing" God. The distinction between philosophy and theology will not be that in the latter the *quid est* of God is grasped, but that the latter leads to a contemplative moment of intimacy with that which remains infinite mystery. Aquinas shows his awareness of this infinite distance in Objection 3, where it is stated that between the human intellect and God there can be no proportion, precisely because there can be none between the finite and the infinite, and thus, the objection states, the human intellect can in no way know God. In his response to this objection Aquinas states that "proportion" involves some sort of agreement between two things, and this agreement may be of two kinds. There is an agreement by reason of two things belonging to the same genus, but this type of proportion is impossible for God and creature. There is another type of "agreement" when two things are associated in a certain order, such as the "proportion," in an extended sense, between maker and the thing made, matter and form, the knower and the knowable. On the part of the human intellect there is a relation of the intellect to God as its cause. However, propter infinitum excessum creatoris super creaturam non est proportio creaturae ad creatorem, ut recipiat influentiam ipsius secundum totam virtutem eius, neque ut ipsum perfecte cognoscat, sicut ipse se ipsum perfecte cognoscit.[57]

So, a proportion is required between the knower and the thing known, but there is no direct proportion possible between the human intellect and God, to the extent that God can be fully known by finite intellect.

Article 3: The First Known by the Human Mind

This article may be treated in passing, as this is a classic and well known theme of Aquinas which he treats in many works. God as such cannot be the first thing known by the human mind because to know God as such, "essentially," is the definition of beatitude. Again, one may note here that this position of Aquinas is somewhat problematic. Aquinas then considers in his response whether the light of the agent intellect, which is not God himself but which is an "influx" of divine light in the human mind, is the first thing known by the human mind. Another way to form this question would be to ask whether the human mind knows itself as the first thing it knows. But the intensity of this light in the human mind is limited, and not of such power that it can immediately know itself. The human mind comes to know by abstracting a form from a material existent. The human mind only comes to know itself when it reflects on the processes of coming to know something else. The human mind only gradually, and with great difficulty, comes to negative knowledge of God.

Article 4: Whether Natural Reason Can Know The Trinity

With regard to the question of whether natural reason can attain knowledge of the Trinity, Aquinas' response is direct and clear:

Responsio. Dicendum quod deum esse trinum et unum est solum creditum, et nullo modo potest demonstrative probari, quamvis ad hoc aliquales rationes non necessariae nec multum probabiles nisi credenti haberi possint. Quod patet ex hoc quod deum non cognoscimus in statu viae nisi ex effectibus, ut ex praedictis patere potest. Et ideo naturali ratione de deo cognoscere non possumus nisi hoc quod percipitur de ipso ex habitudine

---

[57] Ibid., q. 1, a. 2, ad 3 (p. 67). On account of the infinite excess of the creator over the creature, there is no proportion of the creature to the creator which makes it possible to receive from him an influx proportionate to his complete power, or to know him perfectly, as he knows himself perfectly.

effectuum ad ipsum, sicut illa quae designant causalitatem ipsius et eminentiam super causata et quae removent ab ipso imperfectas condiciones effectuum. Trinitas autem personarum non potest percipi ex ipsa causalitate divina, cum causalitas sit communis toti trinitati. Nec etiam dicitur secundum remotionem. Unde nullo modo demonstrative probari potest deum esse trinum et unum.[58]

This will obviously be an important point to keep in mind when it comes to the status of Aquinas' theology of God as Triune. On the level of reason, it will be hard even for the person accepting the articles of faith to find any reasons, or even analogical reasonableness, for the Trinitarian mystery. And yet Aquinas will say in his response to the sixth objection of this Article "Trinitas autem personarum requirit realem distinctionem." This reveals a particular tension: the Trinity is "known" by faith to be beyond reason, and yet faith immediately returns to the domain of conceptual distinctions, even though it realizes that these distinctions are inadequate. Another important point here is that causality is common to the whole Trinity, and this will be of great significance when one considers the "cause" of grace and manners of appropriating the divine Persons. By anticipation one may say that sanctifying grace causes justification, and this grace may be appropriated to the Holy Spirit as cause, but ultimately involves the whole Trinity. It may also be anticipated that the roles of the particular divine Persons in causing sanctifying grace will be impossible to conceptualize.

This mysterious unity of God, and the inability of human reason to consider God conceptually in the totality of the Trinity, and the need of reason, even when enlightened by faith, to consider one aspect at a time, is reflected in the response to the 10th Objection in this Article:

---

[58]   Ibid., q. 1, a. 4, resp. (p. 76). That God is three and one is only known by belief, and it is in no way possible for this to be demonstratively proven by reason, however much to this end some sort of reasons are given, they are neither necessary nor even very likely unless the articles of faith are already held. It is clear that we do not know God in this life except by means of his effects, as can be seen from what has been said [q. 1, a. 2]. Likewise it is not possible for us to know God by natural reason, except for that which is known about God by means of habits of reasoning from effects to God himself as the cause, such as those which designate the causality and eminence of God himself to be beyond the things that God has caused, and which remove from God himself the imperfect conditions of his effects. However, the Trinity of Persons is not able to be perceived by means of reasoning from divine causality itself, because divine causality is common to the total Trinity. Nor can a reasoning to the Trinity of Persons be accomplished by means of remotion. Hence it is in no way possible for reason to demonstratively prove that God is three and one.

[Maurer translates "et ideo naturali ... condiciones effectum" as (p. 32): "Therefore through natural reason we can know about God only what we grasp of him from the relation his effects bear to him, for example, attributes that designate his causality and transcendence over his effects, and that deny of him the imperfections of his effects."]

Dicendum quod omnia, quae in deo sunt, sunt una eius simplex essentia, sed ea, quae in ipso sunt unum, in intellectu nostro sunt multa, et propter hoc intellectus noster potest apprehendere unum istorum sine altero. Inde est quod in statu viae de nullo eorum possumus cognoscere quid est, sed solum an est, et contingit quod cognoscatur, an est unum eorum et non alterum; sicut si aliquis cognosceret, an sit sapientia in deo, non autem an in ipso sit omnipotentia. Et similiter potest ratione naturali sciri an deus sit, non tamen an sit trinus et unus.[59]

It would seem, then, that even in a faithed condition, there is only belief in the "quod sit" of the divine Persons, but no grasp of the "quid sit" of each divine Person, and thus no full understanding of the Trinitarian dynamism, which can only be grasped partially and momentarily by finite consciousness, and not in the totality which is the Trinity.

Question 2: The Manifestation of Divine Knowledge

Article 1: The Use of Reason

Here the fundamental topic of the question involves some shift of terminology. Question 2 is concerned with "De manifestatione divinae cognitionis," the manifestation of knowledge of divine things, and in the first statement, when the outline of the question is introduced, the first Article is referred to as: "Primo: Utrum divina liceat investigando tractare."[60] The "title" of the first Article, which may have been inserted by earlier manuscript copyists, repeats this exactly. But, as the Article begins it states, "Ad primum sic proceditur. Videtur quod divina investigare non liceat argumentando." Now there is simply a difference of meaning between "investigando tractare" and the more specific and strict "investigare ... argumentando." So, there are two problems. First, the shift in the text from "tractare" to "argumentando" and, second, the manner in which "argumentando" should be understood. This proper understanding is important here, as is also the case with the understanding of "argumentativus" in the *Commentary on the Sentences* (I, Question 1, Article 5), and "argumentativa" in the *Summa Theologiae* (I, Question 1, Article 8).

---

[59]   Ibid., ad 10 (p. 79). It is to be said that all things in God are of one, simple essence, but those things that in him are one, are many in our intellect, and on this account our intellect can apprehend one of these things without the other. Therefore in this life we are able to understand the quiddity of none of these things [in God], but only that they exist; and thus it happens that one of them might be known to exist and not another; just as one might know that there is wisdom in God, but not know that there is also omnipotence, and likewise it is possible, by natural reason, to know that God exists, but not to know that he is three and one.

[60]   Ibid., q. 2 (p. 80).

First of all, it would seem advantageous to regard the "liceat investigando tractare" terminology as perhaps a later corruption in the textual tradition. Or, at least one should immediately see that the initial title given the Article does not reflect the actual terminology used in the Article, which starts by using the term "argumentando," and then the term "argumenta" is used in the third objection, while "licet argumentis investigare" is used in the fourth objection, and the term "argumenta" is used once and the term "argumentis" is used three times in the *Sed contra*. So, it is this term rather than "tractare" which is the theme of the Article. The next question here concerns how this term should be understood. As can be seen in the parallel articles in the *Commentary on the Sentences* and the *Summa Theologiae*, although some English translators have rendered this term as "argumentative" or "demonstrative," these meanings are too harsh or too strict for the context of the term. The present Article itself gives a good context for the meaning. In Objection 4 the terms "scrutari" and "ratione" are used; in Objection 5 the term "rationibus"; in Objection 7 "rationis"; and in the *Sed contra* one again finds "rationem," "rationibus," and "ratione." These terms give some evidence that what Aquinas means here is "reasonableness," or "having some reasonableness that aids understanding." And in the corpus and the responses to objections in this Article the term "argumenta" is never used. So, the question is whether it is permitted to investigate divine things, *divina*, in the mode of reason or in a reasonable manner. Aquinas states:

> Responsio. Dicendum quod cum perfectio hominis consistat in coniunctione ad deum, oportet quod homo ex omnibus quae in ipso sunt, quantum possibile est, ad divina admittatur, ut intellectus contemplationi et ratio inquisitioni divinorum vacet, secundum illud Psalmi (72,28): 'Mihi adhaerere deo bonum est.' Et ideo Philosophus in X Ethicorum excludit dictum quorundam qui dicebant quod homo non debeat se intromittere de rebus divinis, sed solum de humanis, sic dicens: 'Oportet autem non secundum suadentes humana sapere hominem entem neque mortalia mortalem, sed in quantum convenit immortale facere et omnia facere ad vivere secundum optimum eorum quae in ipso.'[61]

What is stressed here is not a grasping by reason, but a contemplative engagement with God, in which reason is aware that it can attempt to explore and investigate the domain of God, but in a way that dialectically transcends

---

[61] Ibid., q. 2, a. 1, resp. (p. 82). It is to be said that since the perfection of the human person consists in union with God, it follows that the human person, by all that is within him, and insofar as it is possible, should strive to attain divine things, so that his intellect may contemplate and his reason investigate divine things, according to the Psalm [72.28]: 'It is good for me to adhere to my God.' Hence also the Philosopher in X *Ethics* opposes the saying of those who maintained that man ought not concern himself with divine things, but only about human things, saying, 'One should not follow those who say that being human one is to think of human things, and being mortal of mortal things; rather, insofar as it is fitting, one should make himself immortal and do all things in order to live according to the best of those things that are in him.'

the domain of reason itself. The dialectical tension is most fundamentally expressed in the admonition that the human person's happiness consists "in coniunctione ad deum," and that the human person should "ad divina admittatur," and yet this is qualified, "quantum possibile est."

The rest of the response in this Article continues the qualifications, issuing, as it were, warnings to anyone attempting to investigate the divine. The dangers are presumption, the possible inability of reason to surrender to the deeper cleaving to God by faith, and the possible inability of scientific reason to yield to mystical wisdom:

> Tripliciter tamen contingit in hoc peccare. Primo ex praesumptione qua scilicet aliquis sic ea scrutatur quasi ea perfecte comprehensurus ... . Secundo ex hoc quod in his quae sunt fidei ratio praecedit fidem, non fides rationem, dum scilicet aliquis hoc solum vult credere quod ratione potest invenire, cum debeat esse e converso ... . Tertio ultra modum suae capacitatis ad divinorum perscrutationem se ingerendo, unde dicitur Rom. 12(3): 'Non plus sapere, quam oportet sapere, sed sapere ad sobrietatem,' 'unicuique sicut deus divisit mensuram fidei.'[62]

Thus the stress in the response is certainly on a series of cautionary notes. The first two cautionary notes, indeed strong warnings, concern the relationship of faith and reason. The end-point of theological understanding is not to understand God, as such, but to understand that God is incomprehensible for finite intellect.

And yet there is a constant tension-in-faith for finite intellect. Divine things may be examined by faith seeking understanding, and thus utilizing the natural order of understanding, but with the dialectical limit that perfect comprehension of divine things can never be attained. A constant tension-in-faith arises from the manner in which "faith takes precedence over reason," for this is not a precedence which negates the value of reason, but a precedence which directs reason to its limits, and constantly refuses to be lured by any theory of "double truth." Thus the end-point of theological understanding and contemplation may be the First Truth as God, but in a way that incorporates the natural order of reflection. Additionally, because of the fact that the theologian must be aware of the nature of human cognition, and what it means to perfectly comprehend something, and why it is the case that

---

[62]   Ibid. (pp. 82-83). In a threefold manner, however, one may seriously err in these matters. First by presumption, which is the case when anyone would examine the divine as if he could attain a perfect comprehension of it ... . Second, serious error can arise if, in the investigation of those things which are of faith, reason takes precedence over faith, rather than faith taking precedence over reason, to the point where one would only be willing to believe that which reason was able to discover, when it is the reverse that should be the case ... . Third, serious error can result from an inquiry into the divine which is beyond one's capacity, and hence it is said in Rom. 12[3], 'Not to be more wise than it becomes to be wise, but to be wise unto sobriety,' and 'according as God has divided to each one the measure of faith.'

God cannot be perfectly comprehended by the theologian, the person engaged in theological reflection also needs to reflect on the natural processes and limits of human cognition as such. This is implied in the first point of Aquinas in the above text, and it is likewise implied in the second point: for if the theologian is to understand the ways in which faith may take precedence over reason, then each of the terms involved in this relationship, i.e., faith and reason, must be understood.

Thus by an extended understanding of the implications of the above text, one may say that the end-point of theological understanding retains God as the ultimate "object" ("subject") of search, and yet there is a simultaneous refection on the status of human understanding. The intentionality may be directed to the infinite, but it inevitably returns to the finite for dialectical negation: what is "understood" *is not* that which is understood.

With regard to the second danger enunciated by Aquinas, there is a parallel form of dialectic regarding the relationship of faith and reason. As reason extends itself to its limits, that which was previously of faith is no longer always of faith, but is known naturally. Such can be the case with revealed truths which include naturally knowable truths. But in the domain of faith, reason will ultimately come face-to-face with its limits of understanding, and it is at these limit-points that reason is to open itself before the mystery rather than undertaking judgement which would render the infinite mystery a finite, comprehensible, objective "fact." It seems to be implied in Aquinas' third warning here that it is a divine gift of wisdom which enables the faith-filled person to live in this tension of faith and reason. The limit-discourse of faith may be "understood" or "savored" to a very limited and partial degree by one who is "wise," but this is a different kind of "understanding" or "contemplation" than can be found in Aristotle. The possibilities of a penetration into meaning are even more difficult than in natural metaphysics.

The responses to the last two objections in this Article are particularly profound, and they continue the cautionary notes, while then undertaking a recovery of a theological language, but this language is one of praise and adoration rather than scientific comprehension:

> Ad sextum dicendum quod deus honoratur silentio, non quod nihil de ipso dicatur vel inquiratur, sed quia quidquid de ipso dicamus vel inquiramus, intelligimus nos ab eius comprehensione defecisse, unde dicitur Eccli. 43(32), 'Glorificantes dominum quantumcumque potueritis, supervalebit adhuc.'[63]

---

[63]   Ibid., q. 2, a. 1, ad 6 (p. 84). To the sixth objection it is to be said that God is honored by silence, but not in the sense that nothing may be said of him or no inquiries may be made of him, but simply in the sense that in whatever way we speak of God or make inquiries into God, we understand that our comprehension of God is deficient, hence it is said in Ecclesiastes 43[32], 'Glorify the Lord as much as you are able, yet he will still far exceed' [what you are able].

Ad septimum dicendum quod cum deus in infinitum a creatura distet, nulla creatura movetur in deum, ut ipsi adaequetur vel recipiendo ab ipso vel cognoscendo ipsum. Hoc ergo, quod in infinitum a creatura distat, non est terminus motus creaturae. Sed quaelibet creatura movetur ad hoc quod deo assimiletur plus et plus quantum potest. Et sic etiam humana mens semper debet moveri ad cognoscendum de deo plus et plus secundum modum suum. Unde dicit Hilarius, 'Qui pie infinita persequitur, etsi non contingat aliquando, tamen semper proficiet prodeundo.'[64]

The Sixth Objection is actually based in part on the ending of the *Celestial Hierarchy* of Ps. Dionysius, where it is stated that the highest truth is honored by silence. Aquinas is not absolutely disagreeing with this, but only qualifying it. There is still, for Aquinas, an end-point of silence with regard to that which is in the domain of reason's grasp, but this silence nevertheless breaks forth with the voice of faith, but in a language that is still incomprehensible. The Seventh Objection, which takes as its departure an Aristotelian notion of motion and infinity, does not find a response which solves the dilemma in Aristotelian terms; indeed, Aquinas grants that the finite creature does not fully attain the infinite. Accordingly, there is no end to the theological task of understanding God in even a limited way. There may be partial progress, but the goal is never attained, and it is a progress made more in reverential awe than scientific understanding.

Article 2: Scientific Status

In the Decker edition the title of the Article is, "Utrum de divinis possit esse scientia." In the initial objection the now classic problem of the relationship of "sapientia" and "scientia" is stated. If "sapientia" is that which treats divine things, then the manner of this treatment cannot be "scientia." The objections also state that the "quid est" of God cannot be known, and thus there cannot be a science of God, and that a consideration of divine things cannot be a science because it is not simply a movement of reason, but a movement involving faith. It is also objected, as would be expected, that the first principles of science are *per se nota*, while the articles of faith are not.

---

[64]   Ibid., q. 2, a. 1, ad 7 (pp. 84-85). To the seventh objection it is to be said that God is infinitely distant from creatures, and no creature is moved to God so as to be the equal of God, either in what it receives from God or in or in what it knows of God. From this it follows that because God is infinitely distant from a creature, God cannot be the terminus of the motion of a creature. And yet, every creature is moved to this: that the creature may be assimilated to God, more and more, insofar as this is possible. And it is in this way that the human mind ought to always be moved more and more to knowledge of God, according to the mode of the human mind. And thus it is that Hilary says [*De Trinitate* II, 10], 'He who in pious spirit undertakes the infinite, even though he can not attain it, nevertheless profits by advancing.'

[Here there is an error in Maurer's translation of "Hoc ergo ... creaturae," as "so the goal of the creature's progress is not something infinitely remote from the creature" (p. 39).]

In his response Aquinas states:

> Divinorum notitia dupliciter potest aestimari. Uno modo ex parte nostra, et sic nobis cognoscibilia non sunt nisi per res creatas, quarum cognitionem a sensu accipimus. Alio modo ex natura ipsorum, et sic ipsa sunt ex se ipsis maxime cognoscibilia, et quamvis secundum modum suum non cognoscantur a nobis, tamen a deo cognoscuntur et a beatis secundum modum suum.[65]
>
> Et secundum hoc de divinis duplex scientia habetur. Una secundum modum nostrum, qui sensibilium principia accipit ad notificandum divina, et sic de divinis philosophi scientiam tradiderunt, philosophiam primam scientiam divinam dicentes. Alia secundum modum ipsorum divinorum, ut ipsa divina secundum se ipsa capiantur, quae quidem perfecte in statu viae nobis est impossibilis, sed fit nobis in statu viae quaedam illius cognitionis participatio et assimilatio ad cognitionem divinam, in quantum per fidem nobis infusam inhaeremus ipsi primae veritati propter se ipsam.[66]

This is much more qualified than Aquinas' bold statements in Q. 1, A. 1 of his *Commentary on the Sentences*. One should note that Aquinas is not doing a "proof" here that theology is a science, as Elders claims.[67] What Aquinas is doing is an *ex convenientia* analogy by means of participation, in order to give some sort of reasoned account for human knowledge of the principles of the faith, which are, in some paradoxical manner here, not mediated as such by sensory experience. *The* knowledge of divine truths Aquinas here locates in God and those in Beatific Vision. In the first instance such knowledge is clearly immediate, and in the second instance such knowledge is at least "more immediate" than natural or supernatural knowledge in this life. In the above text Aquinas does *not* argue that access to the principles of sacred theology is absolutely immediate, simply as such - as he appears to argue in the *Commentary on the Sentences*. What Aquinas does argue here, instead, is that there is a *qualified participation*, on the part of the person of faith, in the

---

[65]   Ibid., q. 2. a. 2, resp. (pp. 86-87). Divine truths can be thought of in two ways. One way is from our point of view, and in this way such truths are not knowable except from created things, of which we have knowledge derived from sense experience. The other way is from the nature of the things themselves, for they are, in themselves, maximally knowable, and although they are not known according to their own mode by us, nevertheless they are known by God and the blessed according to their own mode.

[66]   Ibid. (p. 87). And from this it follows that there is a twofold science of the divine. One is according to our mode, for which sensible things serve as principles for coming to knowledge of divine things, and this is the divine science which the philosophers handed down, calling first philosophy divine science. The other mode [of a science of the divine] is according to the divine things themselves, as they are attained [understood, or known, "capiantur"] in themselves, which is a mode that is, indeed, impossible for us to attain perfectly in this life; but there is for us in this life something of that mode of cognition, by means of a participation in and assimilation to a cognition of the divine, inasmuch as through the faith which is infused in us we adhere to the First Truth itself, on account of itself.

[67]   Elders, *Faith and Science: An Introduction to St. Thomas' 'Expositio in Boethii De Trinitate,'* p. 46.

knowledge enjoyed by God and the blessed. This argumentation, which reflects his growing assimilation of the participationist thematics - particularly of Boethius - is *not* one for immediate access to the principles of theology by means of the "light of faith" or "divine inspiration." Rather than immediate access to the principles of theology, Aquinas here argues that the person of faith *cannot* attain perfect (immediate) access to these principles,

> but there is for us in this life *something* of that mode of cognition, by means of a participation in and assimilation to a cognition of the divine, *inasmuch as* through the faith which is infused in us we adhere to the First Truth itself, on account of itself [emphasis added].[68]

Here the stress is still on faith as "infused," but the cognitive content which can result from faith may be understood to be not so much infused as it is a participation in immediate knowledge which still must have recourse to sensory experience in the world. Faith as such, as a principle of the interpretation of experience, may be "immediate," but the knowledge that faith attains is mediated.

The dilemma of Aquinas in the responses to the objections is to argue that such a non-conceptual wisdom, which cannot draw strict conclusions, is still harmoniously related to "science," indeed, as a perfection of science, completing science. The problem is precisely how a non-conceptual, limited attainment of the divine, by means of participation and assimilation, in a Neoplatonic manner independent in some way of sensory experience, can possibly perform the architectonic function of "sapientia." Aquinas argues in the responses that faithed-wisdom is even higher than metaphysical wisdom because such faithed-wisdom is not only about the highest principles, but is *from* the highest principles. The gap here is specifying the exact status of this received wisdom, which is certainly received, in some way, according to the mode of the recipient. In the response to Objection 6, Aquinas further attempts to argue that a faithed-science of the divine can indeed reason to conclusions, and make them evident, indeed, as evident and certain as the principles of faith from which they are derived. Again, it is one thing to assert this in a facile manner, and quite another to specify how the transition to finite language can yield such evident and certain conclusions drawn from principles that are, to reason, the least evident and least certain. Aquinas simply assumes some sort of transition without specifying it.

---

[68]   Aquinas, *Expositio Super Librum Boethii De Trinitate*, q. 2, a. 2, resp. [p. 87].

Article 3: The Utilization of "Philosophy"

As is the case in the *Commentary on the Sentences* and the *Summa Theologiae*, when Aquinas refers to the use of "philosophia," he means the entire range of natural, rational knowledge. In this *Expositio*, he argues that because of the relationship of nature and grace, theology is free to make use of philosophy, and theology actually perfects philosophy:

> Dicendum quod dona gratiarum hoc modo naturae adduntur quod eam non tollunt, sed magis perficiunt; unde et lumen fidei, quod nobis gratis infunditur, non destruit lumen naturalis rationis divinitus nobis inditum. Et quamvis lumen naturale mentis humanae sit insufficiens ad manifestationem eorum quae manifestantur per fidem, tamen impossibile est quod ea, quae per fidem traduntur nobis divinitus, sint contraria his quae sunt per naturam nobis indita. Oporteret enim alterum esse falsum; et cum utrumque sit nobis a deo, deus nobis esset auctor falsitatis quod est impossibile. Sed magis cum in imperfectis inveniatur aliqua imitatio perfectorum, in ipsis, quae per naturalem rationem cognoscuntur, sunt quaedam similitudines eorum quae per fidem sunt tradita ... .[69]
>
> Sic ergo in sacra doctrina philosophia possumus tripliciter uti. Primo ad demonstrandum ea quae sunt praeambula fidei, quae necesse est in fide scire, ut ea quae naturalibus rationibus de deo probantur, ut deum esse, deum esse unum et alia huiusmodi vel de deo vel de creaturis in philosophia probata, quae fides supponit. Secundo ad notificandum per aliquas similitudines ea quae sunt fidei, sicut Augustinus in libro De trinitate utitur multis similitudinibus ex doctrinis philosophicis sumptis ad manifestandum trinitatem. Tertio ad resistendum his quae contra fidem dicuntur sive ostendendo ea esse falsa sive ostendendo ea non esse necessaria.[70]

---

[69]   Ibid., q. 2, a. 3, resp. (p. 94). It is to be said that the gifts of grace are added to nature in such a way that they do not destroy it, but perfect it; and hence also the light of faith, which is gratuitously infused into us, does not destroy the natural light of reason which the divinity has given to us. For although the natural light of the human mind is insufficient for the manifestation of those things which are manifested by faith, nevertheless it is impossible that those things which are handed on [revealed] to us by the divinity should be contrary to those things which are instilled in us by nature. In such a case, one would be false, and since both kinds [of truths] are ours from God, God would be the author of falsity, which is impossible. Rather, it is much more the case that since in imperfect things there is found some sort of imitation of perfect things, in those things which are known by means of natural reason, there are certain sorts of similitudes to those things which are handed on [revealed] through faith.

[70]   Ibid. (pp. 94-95). It follows from this that *sacra doctrina* is able to make a threefold use of philosophy. First, to demonstrate those things which are preambles of the faith, which are necessary to know in faith, such as those things which by natural reasons can be proved, such as the existence of God, that God is one, and other such things about God or about creatures which are proven in philosophy, and which faith presupposes. The second way is to give a notion, by means of some similitudes to those things which are of the faith, as Augustine, in his book, *De Trinitate* [9-12, 14-14], utilized many similitudes taken from the doctrines of the philosophers in order to manifest the Trinity. The third way is to refute those things which are said contrary to the faith, either in showing them to be false or showing that they are not necessary.

In the response to Objection 5 in this Article, Aquinas makes some interesting observations on the problematic transition from "symbolic" to "argumentative" theology. In the fifth objection it had been stated, with reference to Isaiah 1 - in which innkeepers were admonished for mixing water with wine:

> Saecularis sapientia frequenter in scriptura per aquam significatur, sapientia vero divina per vinum ... . Ergo vituperandi sunt doctores qui sacrae doctrinae philosophica documenta admiscent.[71]

The response is:

> Dicendum quod ex tropicis locutionibus non est sumenda argumentatio, ut dicit Magister 11 [sic. XI] distinctione III Sententiarum, et Dionysius dicit in Epistula ad Titum quod symbolica theologia non est argumentativa, et praecipue cum illa expositio non sit alicuius auctoris. Et tamen potest dici quod quando alterum duorum transit in dominium alterius, non reputatur mixtio, sed quando utrumque a sua natura alteratur. Unde illi qui utuntur philosophicis documentis in sacra doctrina redigendo in obsequium fidei, non miscent aquam vino, sed aquam convertunt in vinum.[72]

One must admit that Aquinas again makes matters appear rather simple, but it would perhaps help if he had given a more specific recipe for such alchemical transformations. What should also be noted is that his language about the "utilization" of philosophy by sacred doctrine gives the impression that *sacra doctrina* is somehow constituted as a reflective reality in human consciousness prior to and independently of an engagement with natural knowledge.

Article 4: Obscurity and Veiledness

In this Article, Aquinas again moderates the view that he at times expresses, according to which there is a rather "clear" participation in God's self-knowledge possible in this life because of the "immediate" illumination of the

---

[71] Ibid., q. 2, a. 3, ob 5 (p. 91). Secular wisdom is frequently signified in Scripture by water, but divine wisdom by wine ... . Therefore [sacred] doctors are blameworthy who mix sacred doctrine with philosophical learning ["documenta"].

[72] Ibid., q. 2, a. 3, ad 5 (p. 96). It is to be said that from figurative speech, no conclusive argument can be drawn, as the Master [Lombard] says in Distinction 11 of III *Sentences*, and Dionysius also says in his *Letter to Titus* that symbolic theology is not argumentative, especially when he who writes the exposition is not any sort of authority. Nevertheless it can be said that when one of two things passes into the domain of the other, the result is not considered a mixture, except when the nature of both is altered. Hence those who use philosophical doctrines in *sacra doctrina* in such a way as to subject them to the service of the faith, do not mix water with wine, but change water into wine.

divine Light of revelation. In this final Article of the Question, there is a parallel to Aquinas' cautionary notes at the conclusion of his "Prologue" to the *Sentences*. Here in this Article, the initial, general objection is stated as: "Videtur quod divina in scientia fidei non sunt obscuritate verborum velanda,"[73] and this is printed as a general introduction to the six specific objections which follow, rather than being a part of Objection 1 as such. The first five objections are all based on biblical texts,[74] while the last objection is based on Augustine's statement that sermons should be clear and easily understood.[75]

> Responsio. Dicendum quod verba docentis ita debent esse moderata ut proficiant, non noceant audienti. Quaedam autem sunt quae audita nemini nocent, sicut ea quae omnes scire tenentur; et talia non sunt occultanda, sed manifeste omnibus proponenda. Quaedam vero sunt quae proposita manifeste auditoribus nocent; quod quidem contingit dupliciter. Uno modo, si arcana fidei infidelibus fidem abhorrentibus denudentur. Eis enim venirent in derisum; et propter hoc dominus dicit Matth. 7(6): 'Nolite sanctum dare canibus' ... . Secundo, quando aliqua subtilia rudibus proponuntur, ex quibus perfecte non comprehensis materiam sumunt errandi ... . Haec ergo ab his, quibus nocent, occultanda sunt.[76]

Thus there is a type of veiledness and obscurity necessary, even for men and women of faith, in that a knowledge of actual truth could be too scandalous for their comprehension to bear; and such truths are best kept veiled in silence - or in multiple paradoxes of structures which superficially give content, but which ultimately result in conceptual vacuity.

In this response Aquinas also gives a possible insight into the influence of this factor on the structure and content of his own written works, and in this response Aquinas is also citing Augustine as an authority with whom he agrees on this point. In oral communication, it is possible for the speaker to judge the wisdom of the hearers, and avoid the presentation of barely comprehensible truths to those who would find them an unbearable scandal. But in published works, an author cannot know the wisdom of his or her

---

[73]   Ibid., q. 1, a. 4 (p. 97).
[74]   Prov. 14,6; Eccl. 4,28; Prov. 11,26; Mt. 10,27; Rom. 1,14, and Wis. 7,13.
[75]   Augustine, *De Doctrina Christiana* IV.
[76]   Aquinas, *Expositio Super Librum Boethii De Trinitate*, q. 2, a. 4, resp. (pp. 98-99). I answer that the words of a teacher ought to be so moderated that they result to the profit and not to the detriment of the one hearing him. Now, there are certain things which on being heard harm no one, as are the truths which all are held responsible to know; and such ought not to be hidden but openly proposed to all. But there are others which if openly presented cause harm in those hearing them, and this can occur for two reasons. First, if the secret truths of faith are revealed to infidels who detest the faith, so that the truths of the faith come to be derided by them. On this account it is said in Mt. 7[6]: 'Give not that which is holy to dogs' ... . Second, if any subtleties are proposed to uncultivated people, these folk may find in the imperfect comprehension of these subtleties matter for error ... . These truths, therefore, ought to be hidden from those to whom they might do harm.

readers, for a book can fall into the hands of anyone. Thus Aquinas holds that an author may be bound to express some profound and difficult truths in a veiled way with obscure words, so that they may profit the wise who read them, but will not be comprehended by intellectually uncultivated - though faithed - readers, for whom such truths might cause a scandal.

One may accordingly only speculate whether Aquinas' own *Commentary on the Sentences*, his *Expositio* of the *De Trinitate*, as well as his *Summa Contra Gentiles*, and *Summa Theologiae* were in fact written with this in mind. Perhaps one must search for subtle and veiled clues of structure and terminological relationships if one is to read more accurately the fuller intention and personal understanding of Aquinas. In the judgement of the present author, it is the case that Aquinas quite frequently presents formulations that seem to have clarity of surface structure and terminology, but these are structures for novices, because Aquinas thought that his own, overpowering *agnosia* in faith would cause too much scandal and harm to those who were lacking refined cultivation in philosophical knowledge and maturity of faith.

Question 3: On Those Things that Pertain to the Faith

In Question 3 Aquinas addresses what pertains to the faith, in four articles: 1) whether faith is necessary, 2) how faith is related to religion, 3) whether the true faith is called Catholic, and 4) whether the confession of the true faith is Trinitarian. Here the first two articles are of more concern for the status and method of theology, though the last two also have some elements of importance for the focus at hand.

Article 1: The Necessity of Faith

In the response to Article 1 Aquinas makes an interesting distinction between faith and "understanding":

> Responsio. Dicendum quod fides habet aliquid commune cum opinione et aliquid cum scientia et intellectu, ratione cuius ponitur media inter scientiam et opinionem ab Hugone de Sancto Victore. Cum scientia siquidem et intellectu commune habet certum et fixum assensum, in quo ab opinione differt, quae accipit alterum contrariorum cum formidine alterius, et a dubitatione quae fluctuat inter duo contraria. Sed cum opinione commune habet quod est de rebus quae non sunt intellectui pervia, in quo differt a scientia et intellectu.[77]

---

[77] Ibid., q. 3, a. 1, resp. (pp. 109-110). It is to be said that faith has something in common with opinion and something in common with scientific knowledge and understanding, by reason

Now a dilemma is immediately proposed, for it is claimed that faith is certain knowledge involving firm assent, and yet what is assented to is not really grasped or understood.

Aquinas then argues that faith is concerned with God, who is most knowable in himself, but not evidently knowable on the part of the human intellect, because of the defect of the human intellect; and thus faith is necessary, though it does not provide scientific knowledge or complete understanding. This de-emphasis on the scientific and understanding aspects of faith reflects an admirable humility on the part of Aquinas; but then, in the response to the objection, Aquinas immediately reintroduces a dialectical counterpoint in order to express that while faith is not science or understanding, it is beyond science and understanding. The thrust of the first objection is that faith cannot be necessary since it pertains to what is beyond human nature and human reason. Aquinas responds:

> Ad primum ergo dicendum quod licet ea quae sunt fidei sint maiora homine naturae viribus consideratis, non sunt tamen maiora homine divino lumine elevato. Et ideo non est necesse homini, ut huiusmodi propria virtute quaerat, sed est ei necesse, ut divina revelatione ea *cognoscat* [emphasis added].[78]

In this Article, Aquinas constructs a paradox of words, perhaps intentionally veiling his meaning, as he attempts to argue that faith is not, strictly speaking, *scientia* or *intellectus*, but to have faith still means that the believer *cognoscat* - something. One cannot conceptually fathom what it means to know, but to know without a scientific knowledge, in a manner that is not opinion, and without, as Aquinas here stresses, real understanding.

Objection 4 in this Article is also quite significant. The objection states that whenever there is acceptance of knowledge without judgement, error easily arises. But in matters of faith, judgement is impossible. So it would seem best to avoid such matters.

---

of which faith is considered between scientific knowledge and mere opinion, according to Hugh of St. Victor [*De Sacramentis Christianae Fidei* p. 10 c. 2, PL 176, 330 C]. Faith has in common with scientific knowledge and understanding the fact that it has certain and fixed assent, and in this it differs from opinion, which accepts one of two opposite views, though with fear that the other might be true; and faith differs from doubt, which fluctuates between two contraries. But in common with opinion faith is concerned with things that are not intellectually clear, and in this respect faith differs from scientific knowledge and understanding.

[78] Ibid., q. 3, a. 1, ad 1 (p. 113). To the first objection it is to be said that although matters of faith are above humanity, considered according to its natural powers, matters of faith are not above human nature when it is elevated by divine light. Hence it is not necessary that the human person seek out such truths by his own power, but it is necessary that the human person *knows* them by divine revelation [emphasis added].

The response to this objection is quite extraordinary, at least in terms of Lonergan's[79] analysis of understanding and judgement in the thought of Aquinas, as well as in terms of a dialectical shift in the texts of Aquinas toward an emphasis on will over intellect.

In his response Aquinas states that when the mind engages in assent, something must move the mind to do so. Some acts of assent result from clear demonstration, while others result from mere opinion, but there are also some acts of assent which are moved by a special light which Aquinas here terms the "habitus fidei." Aquinas then stretches his point in a dialectical exaggeration which oversimplifies matters. With regard to this "habitus fidei" Aquinas states:

> Quod quidem sufficientius est ad inducendum quam aliqua demonstratio, per quam etsi numquam falsum concludatur, frequenter tamen in hoc homo fallitur, quod putat esse demonstrationem quae non est.[80]

The obvious dilemma which Aquinas should face in this reasoning is that it is also frequently the case that those who presumably are enlightened by the habit of faith also have historically arrived at conclusions they thought were demonstrated as following from faith, and yet these conclusions were not of such a status. What Aquinas ignores here is the transition from a participation in the Truth, by means of the light of faith, to the application of this in finite language; what he ignores is the finite order of the meaning of the participated truth to which one assents. Aquinas fails to distinguish adequately enough, in this dialectical insistence, the light of faith as such and the engagement of this light with the finite order so that finite language and judgements may be made:

> Lumen autem fidei, quod est quasi quaedam sigillatio primae veritatis in mente, non potest fallere, sicut nec deus potest decipi vel mentiri, unde hoc lumen sufficit ad iudicandum.[81]

What Aquinas does here is conflate the meanings of a participation in the First Truth, and the status of this First Truth Itself. The light of faith is a finite, although supernatural, participation in the First Truth. Neither its

---

[79] B. Lonergan, "Theology and Understanding," *Collection: Papers by Bernard Lonergan*, ed. F. Crowe (New York: Herder and Herder, 1968), pp. 121-141.

[80] Aquinas, *Expositio Super Librum Boethii De Trinitate*, q. 3, a. 1, ad 4 (p. 114). [This special light which is the habit of faith] is more sufficient for inducing [assent] than any demonstration, for though through the latter [in genuine demonstration] no false conclusion is reached, nevertheless it is frequently the case that humans err in this, in thinking that something is demonstrated which is not.

[81] Ibid. The light of faith, which is, as it were, a kind of impression of the first truth upon the mind, cannot deceive, any more than God can be deceived or lie, and therefore this light suffices for making judgement.

participation nor its supernatural status guarantees that judgements made in the finite order concerning the meaning of God cannot be inaccurate, or even gross failures. It is one thing to say that the First Truth cannot err, and another thing to say that a participation in the First Truth cannot err. The next thing to note here is that Aquinas makes a surprisingly strong conclusion: "Hoc lumen sufficit ad iudicandum." Now, Aquinas would normally not say that the light of faith would ever enable finite intellect to *judge* the First Truth, which is totally beyond the comprehension of finite intellect. One does not judge the truths of faith, so much as accept them. Further, even if one interprets Aquinas here to be saying that the light of faith suffices for making judgements in the realm of finite language and the created order as to the participated and finite meaning of revelation and how this should be applied in the created order, the manner in which such judgements could be made is utterly mysterious.

It is perhaps because of this particular dilemma that in Aquinas' next statement in the text, he addresses the customary issue of intellect and will, but in a manner of dialectical opposition to his customary emphasis on the intellect. He argues that the habit of faith does not move one (to assent and to judgement?) by way of intellectual understanding, "viam intellectus," but by way of the will "viam voluntatis." Still, the remaining problem will be how "judgement" is made if what is assented to is itself not understood, either by the intellect, or in some manner of "understanding" perhaps more properly associated with "will."

Article 2: The Distinction of Faith and Religion

Here the objections are that faith should not be distinguished from religion, while Aquinas' final conclusion is that faith is not materially different from religion, but it is formally different.

While most of this Article is not directly pertinent to the present concerns, it is worthy of note that it is here that Aquinas employs the term "mens," as referring to the totality of the mind, consisting of both intellect and will, rather than simply referring to "intellectus," as "intellect." This use of the term "mens" is in continuity with his reflections on intellect and will in the previous Article.

In the response of Article 2 Aquinas states:

Ipse autem qui colitur, cum sit spiritus, non potest corpore, sed sola mente contingi. Et sic cultus ipsius principaliter in mentis actibus consistit, quibus mens ordinatur in deum.[82]

Here again, although the indication is perhaps subtle, Aquinas is referring to *acts* of the mind, which include acts of intellect and will, rather than referring to the act of the intellect simply as such. The point is simply that the human mind is ordered to come to God through the immaterial and immanent acts of knowledge and love which characterize human being. The point of value here is the admirable balance and integration which Aquinas reflects regarding these two faculties, though the full implications of this interactive balance are not to be found in the *Expositio* of the *De Trinitate*, but more in the *Summa Contra Gentiles* and the *Summa Theologiae*.

There then follows an Article 3 which addresses the catholicity of the Christian faith, and a final Article 4 which is devoted to the notions of "equality," as they could apply to the Trinity of Divine Persons. The notion of "plurality" proposed is directly derived from Boethius, but the subtle *agnosia* in Boethius' recognition of the impossibility of predicating "number" of the divinity is not particularly exploited by Aquinas, whose more "moderate" position will recognize that number cannot be predicated properly of God, but who appears somewhat less radical than Boethius in his treatment of this theme.

Question 4: The Cause of Plurality

Question 4 explores philosophical understandings of plurality. This question addresses four issues: 1) whether otherness is the cause of plurality, 2) whether a difference of accidents causes a diversity in number, 3) whether two bodies exist, or can be thought to exist, in the same place, and 4) whether a difference in place has some bearing on a difference in number.[83] The definitions, arguments, and conclusions are almost entirely philosophical, and

---

[82]   Ibid., q. 3, a. 2, resp. (p. 118). He himself who is reverenced [i.e., God as reverenced in religious veneration], since he is a spirit, cannot be contacted by the body, but only by the mind, and so worship of him consists chiefly in acts of the mind by which the mind is oriented to God.

[83]   See discussion and bibliography in J. Wippel, "Thomas Aquinas on the Distinction and Derivation of the Many from the One: A Dialectic between Being and Nonbeing," *The Review of Metaphysics* 38 (1985), 563-590. See also U. Degl' Innocenti, "Il pensiero di san Tommaso sul principio d'individuazione," *Divus Thomas* (Piacenza) 45 (1942), 35-81; J. Gracia, *Introduction to the Problem of Individuation in the Early Middle Ages* (Washington, D.C.: The Catholic University of America Press, 1984); I. Klinger, *Das Prinzip der Individuation bei Thomas von Aquin* (Munsterschwarzach: Vier-Turme, 1964); H. Weidemann, *Metaphysik und Sprache. Eine sprachphilosophische Untersuchung zu Thomas von Aquin und Aristoteles* (Freiburg-Munich: Karl Alber, 1975), esp. pp. 47-61.

the end result is to leave the reader wondering how Aquinas would have made the explicit connections in Trinitarian theology.

Plurality is said to result from the fact that something is divisible or is actually divided.[84] The primary source of plurality is negation; so that otherness is the source of plurality.[85] In composit substances there are only three causes of diversity: matter, form, and the composit of the two.[86] A form is rendered individual by being received in matter; matter is the subject of dimensions, which are accidents, and thus matter is the principle of such unity and plurality. Physical bodies are prevented from being in the same place by the nature of matter.[87] Thus diversity in number is caused by matter existing under dimensions; differences of accidents arising from matter bring about diversity in number.[88] The diversity in number of incorporeal substances can only follow from their difference in species of incorporeal substances.[89]

In this Question, Aquinas does not directly address several major problems. There is no way in which plurality in the Trinity can be based on divisibility of essence or species. There also cannot be plurality in the Trinity on the basis of divisibility or actual division of substance, or matter, or form. The Divine Persons cannot be distinct in themselves in that the One Form is rendered distinct in three different individuations in matter; likewise the Divine Persons cannot be distinct on the basis of accidental dimensions, and they cannot be considered "species" in a "genus" of God, and they cannot be considered to occupy a "space" to the exclusion of one another. Since the Boethian source of plurality is "otherness," there is no intelligible manner in which the One Essence of the Divine Persons can result in plurality.

Now, Maurer states that in Q. 4, A. 1, "St. Thomas accepts the Boethian analysis of otherness as far as it goes, but he makes a deeper study of the axiom, 'the source of plurality is otherness.'"[90] But one may question whether Aquinas actually makes such a "deeper study," or whether in fact he simplifies the dialectical limitations in Boethian discourse. Maurer, and others - e.g., Nicolas, have a tendency to objectivize metaphysical analogies in Aquinas, in an effort to make intelligible what ultimately cannot be made intelligible in this life. At least Maurer does acknowledge that Aquinas did

---

[84]   Aquinas, *Expositio Super Librum Boethii De Trinitate*, q. 4, a. 1, resp.; cf. Aristotle, *Metaphysics* 10.3.

[85]   Aquinas, *Expositio Super Librum Boethii De Trinitate*, q. 4, a. 1, resp.

[86]   Ibid., q. 4, a. 2, resp.

[87]   Ibid., q. 4, a. 3, resp.

[88]   Ibid., q. 4, a. 4, resp.

[89]   Ibid., ad 5.

[90]   Maurer, *Thomas Aquinas: Faith, Reason and Theology*, p. xxv.

Thomas does not apply his analysis of otherness to the Trinity, no doubt because he did not complete his commentary on the treatise of Boethius. Had he done so, he would have had occasion to draw important consequences regarding the Trinity from his deepened notion of otherness. We can surmise what some of them would have been, however, if we examine his trinitarian doctrine in his later writings.[91]

But, Maurer thus tries to homogenize Aquinas and avoid the difficult dialectical tensions in the present *Expositio*. Maurer's interpretation is more stereotypically neoscholastic in this regard:

Thomas finds the general term 'distinction' most appropriate to express the otherness of persons in the Trinity [*De Potentia* 9, 8 ad 2]. As for the nature of this distinction, he specifies that they are distinct not in the order of essence of being but in the order of relation. As Boethius [*De Trinitate* 6] says, following Augustine [*De Trinitate* 5.11-14], 'relation brings about the Trinity.'[92]

What Boethius said, in fact, and what Aquinas and Maurer both fail to fully address is:

Sed quoniam nulla relatio ad se ipsum referri potest, idciro quod ea secundum se ipsum est praedicatio quae relatione caret, facta quidem est trinitatis numerositas in eo quod est praedicatio relationis ... . Nam omne aequale aequali aequale est et simile simili simile est et idem ei quod est idem idem est; et similis est relatio in trinitate patris ad filium et utriusque ad spiritum sanctum ut eius quod est idem ad id quod est idem. Quod si id in cunctis aliis rebus non potest inveniri, facit hoc cognata caducis rebus alteritas. Nos vero nulla imaginatione diduci sed simplici intellectu erigi et ut quidque intellegi potest ita aggredi etiam intellectu oportet.[93]

In this original line of thought of Boethius, the result is the notion of plurality in the Trinity is totally incomprehensible to reason. Nevertheless, in Question 4 the only properly Trinitarian statement Aquinas makes is:

---

[91] Ibid., p. xxvii.

[92] Ibid., p. xxviii.

[93] Boethius, *De Trinitate* (pp. 28, 30). But since no relation can be affirmed of one subject alone, since a predication referring to one substance is a predication without relation, the manifoldness of the Trinity is secured through the category of relation ... . For equals are equal, like are like, identicals are identical, each with other, and the relation of Father to Son, and of both to the Holy Spirit is a relation of identicals. But if a relation of this kind cannot be found in all other things, this is because of the otherness natural to all perishable, transitory objects. But we ought not to be led astray by imagination, but raised up by pure understanding and, so far as anything can be understood, to this point also we should approach it with our understanding.

Ad primum ergo dicendum quod dupliciter aliqua propositio potest dici non intelligibilis. Uno modo ex parte intelligentis qui deficit intellectu, sicut haec propositio: 'in tribus personis divinis est una essentia.'[94]

Aquinas simply states that this proposition itself need not imply contradiction; if it seems to imply contradiction the knower attempting to understand it only lacks understanding.[95] The second way in which a proposition can be unintelligible is that the proposition itself may contain a contradiction; and Aquinas seems to hold the position that Trinitarian doctrinal propositions in human language do not, in themselves, contain or imply any contradictions. But in this unfinished *Expositio,* just what the "understanding" is that enables such propositions to be "understood," is not clarified by Aquinas. At the conclusion of his Tractate II, Boethius stated only "if possible, reconcile faith and reason."[96] The tendency in Aquinas, for complex historical reasons arising from Latin Averroism, was to insist on a much clearer reconciliation than may well be possible.

Question 5: The Division of The Speculative Sciences

As has been seen, in Section II of his *De Trinitate*, Boethius proposes a threefold division of the speculative sciences, i.e., physics, mathematics, and "theology," the latter meaning, for Boethius, metaphysics; for as Boethius states it, this "theology" is concerned with what does not exist in motion and cannot be imagined, but can only be approached with intellectual concepts. Aquinas' Question 5 treats this division of the sciences, while his Question 6 is concerned with their respective methods.[97]

There is an immediate tension here, for in Aquinas' brief "Introduction" to this section of his *Expositio,* he correctly interprets Boethius to be concerned

---

[94]   Aquinas, *Expositio Super Librum Boethii De Trinitate*, q. 4, a. 3, ad 1 (p. 151). A proposition can be said to be unintelligible in two ways. In one way on the part of the knower who lacks understanding. An example is the proposition: 'In the three divine persons there is one essence.'

[95]   Ibid.

[96]   Cf. Boethius, *Consolation of Philosophy*, V, 3 (Loeb Edition, p. 403): "Quaenam discors foedera rerum causa resolvit? Quis tanta deus veris statuit bella duobus, ut quae carptim singula constent eadem nolint mixta iugari?" ("What cause discordant breaks the world's compact? What god sets strife so great, between two truths, that those same things which stand, alone and separate, together mixed, refuse to be so yoked?")

[97]   For an excellent discussion and analysis of these themes see J. Wippel, "Metaphysics and 'Separatio' in Thomas Aquinas," *Metaphysical Themes in Thomas Aquinas* (Washington, D.C.: The Catholic University of America Press, 1984), pp. 69-104. For one of the most thorough studies on this topic, see the dissertation by J. Wagner, which was directed by Wippel, "A Study of What Can and Cannot be Determined about 'Separatio' as it is Discussed in the Works of Thomas Aquinas" (Ph.D. Dissertation, The Catholic University of America, The School of Philosophy, Studies in Philosophy no. 278, 1979).

with a theological investigation of the Christian doctrine of the Trinity. The initial tension is that while Boethius never actually analyzes theological methodology, he does presuppose the validity of using metaphysical distinctions in theology. What Boethius also does is to apply metaphysical method to his own Trinitarian theology, especially in the manner in which he clarifies terms such as "nature," "substance," "relation," and "person." However, one must recall that Boethius' own reflections on the status of theological knowledge are very qualified, and his position is ultimately one of a profound *agnosia*. What Boethius does is not so much an explicit reflection on the relationship of metaphysics and Trinitarian theology, as assume that this is simply the way to do theology. His goal, as he stated at the end of his own Tractate II, was to "if possible, reconcile faith and reason." But Boethius does not offer a fully explicit methodological reflection on the relationship of metaphysics and Christian theology. And even in Aquinas' unfinished *Expositio* there are only some initial indications given, and the stress is so much on the methodologies of the rational sciences that many scholars have simply overlooked the fact that Aquinas does also deal with Christian theology. For example, Maurer remarked that:

> The nature of theology as the science of Sacred Scripture is not considered in these Questions [V and VI]. They contain a few incidental remarks about it, but these are only to contrast it with metaphysics. St. Thomas had already treated the science of Sacred Scripture in the earlier Questions (I-III). Here his perspective is that of the sciences attainable through the natural light of reason.[98]

But, Aquinas is actually doing more than merely contrasting Christian theology and metaphysics in Questions 5 and 6. As Boethius himself had done, Aquinas is applying the limits of understanding which effect metaphysical knowledge to the limits of understanding possible in theological knowledge, in a profoundly faith-filled *agnosia*. Further, it is clearly the case, for Aquinas, that Christian theology has some sort of status as a "speculative science," and in these Questions 5 and 6 he was attempting to develop the similarities and distinctions between sacred theology and metaphysics.

Question 5 consists of four articles which address: 1) whether the threefold division of the speculative sciences is suitable, 2) whether natural philosophy treats things that are in motion and matter, 3) whether mathematics studies things viewed apart from motion and matter, and 4) whether divine science, *divina scientia*, or metaphysics, is concerned with those things that are without notion and matter. With regard to the title of this fourth article it

---

[98]   A. Maurer, "Introduction" to *St. Thomas Aquinas: The Division and Methods of the Sciences. Questions V and VI of his Commentary on the 'De Trinitate' of Boethius*, trans. with Introduction and Notes by A. Maurer, 3rd rev. ed. (Toronto: The Pontifical Institute of Mediaeval Studies, 1963), p. viii.

should be noted that for Aquinas, *divina scientia* means "first philosophy" or "metaphysics," as distinguished from *sacra doctrina* or "Christian theology." And so, in the formal structure of this Question, the possible relationship is not yet addressed.

Article 1: The Threefold Division

The very first objection is pertinent, for here it is stated that the division of the speculative sciences should not be physics, mathematics, and divine science, but "science," "understanding," and "wisdom," because these are the three speculative habits which perfect the contemplative part of the soul.[99]

In his response Aquinas holds that the theoretical sciences are distinguished according to the essential distinctions among their objects rather than simply on the type of speculative habit involved, and this is then further clarified in his response to the first objection:

> Ad primum ergo dicendum quod Philosophus in VI Ethicorum determinat de habitibus intellectualibus, in quantum sunt virtutes intellectuales. Dicuntur autem virtutes, in quantum perficiunt in sua operatione. 'Virtus enim est quae bonum facit habentem et opus eius bonum reddit'; et ideo secundum quod diversimode perficitur per huiusmodi habitus speculativos, diversificat huiusmodi virtutes. Est autem alius modus quo pars animae speculativa perficitur per intellectum, qui est habitus principiorum, quo aliqua ex se ipsis nota fiunt et quo cognoscuntur conclusiones ex huiusmodi principiis demonstratae, sive demonstratio procedat ex causis inferioribus, sicut est in scientia, sive ex causis altissimis, ut in sapientia. Cum autem distinguuntur scientiae ut sunt habitus quidam, oportet quod penes obiecta distinguantur, id est penes res, de quibus sunt scientiae. Et sic distinguuntur hic et in VI Metaphysicae tres partes philosophiae speculativae.[100]

Here Aquinas repeats his frequent position that "understanding" is a habit of principles. The slight twist in this text is that he allows for a process of

---

[99]   Cf. Aristotle, *Nicomachean Ethics*, VI.

[100]   Aquinas, *Expositio Super Librum Boethii De Trinitate*, q. 5, a. 1, ad 1 (pp. 166-167). To the first objection it is to be said that Aristotle, in *Nicomachean Ethics* VI, makes a determination regarding the intellectual habits, insofar as they are intellectual virtues. Now, they are called virtues insofar as they perfect [the intellect] in its operation, for 'virtue is, indeed, that which makes its possessor good and renders his work good' [*Nic. Ethic*. II, c. 5]; and for this reason Aristotle distinguishes between virtues of this sort inasmuch as speculative habits perfect [the intellect] in different ways. In one way the speculative part of the soul is perfected by understanding, which is the habit of principles, through which some things become known of themselves. In another way it is perfected by a habit through which conclusions demonstrated from these principles are known, whether the demonstration proceeds from inferior causes, as in science, or from the highest causes, as in wisdom. But when the sciences are differentiated insofar as they are habits, they must be distinguished according to their objects, that is, according to the things which the sciences treat. And it is in this way that both here and in the *Metaphysics* VI that Aristotle distinguishes three parts of speculative philosophy.

demonstration in "wisdom," with such a process being distinguished from "science" only in that "wisdom" proceeds from a knowledge of the highest causes. He does not discuss here the contemplative function of "wisdom," though this may be assumed. He also repeats that the sciences should be differentiated according to their objects, and not simply according to their habits, and this is obviously necessary if there is to be a unique sacred theology as distinguished from divine science or metaphysics. But the distinction is very difficult to draw, at least in some respects, for although it is not addressed specifically here, the problem remains that God cannot be directly the "object" of any finite science, and the manner in which the God of revelation could somehow be the "object" of a "science" is even more difficult to specify than how the One God, as the First Cause, above being, could be in some way the "object" of metaphysics.

Article 3: Objects Not in Matter or Motion

The initial problem addressed in this Article is whether mathematics treats what initially exists in matter and motion, but then abstracts from these conditions. In this Article, initial distinctions regarding *separatio* are presented.

In his response, Aquinas states that the intellect, "intellectus," has two operations, as Aristotle[101] stated: the first operation is the "understanding of indivisibles" ("intelligentia indivisibilium"), by which the intellect knows *what* a thing is. And thus this operation is concerned with the essence of a thing, the *quid est*. The second operation is the way in which the intellect joins and divides things, i.e., in forming affirmative and negative propositions. While the first operation is concerned with the "nature" of a thing, the second is concerned with the "being," "esse," of a thing, and it is this second operation which is usually termed "judgement" in general thomistic literature,[102] while the first operation is usually termed "simple apprehension."[103]

The summary point of importance here is that in the second operation, considered as the negative judgement of *separatio*, there is not quidditative knowledge of a thing, but only knowledge that it exists, *quod est*, even though this second operation involves "composition or division," i.e., affirmative or negative propositions. Further, since it is a negative judgement,

[101] Aristotle, *De Caelo et Mundo*, III, 1.

[102] See A. McNicholl, "On Judging," *The Thomist* 38 (1974), 789-825; "On Judging Existence," *The Thomist* 43 (1979), 507-580; J. Owens, "Aquinas on Knowing Existence," *The Review of Metaphysics* 29 (1976), 670-690.

[103] Cf. Aquinas, *Summa Theologiae*, I, q. 85, a. 1, ad 1; *In De Anima*, Lectio XI; *In Post. Anal.*, Prolog.

it is knowledge only that a thing *is*, but not in the same way that proper objects of the intellect, in the sensible world, have existence. And this is the type of judgement specific to divine science.[104] This type of judgement is not an "abstraction," simply as such, but only in the more general sense of a "removal," though specifically by way of negation. Its application to divine science is that by means of *separatio* the intellect acknowledges and asserts that "being," "esse," need not be identified with material, sensible, changing "being," or even "being" of a particular or determined kind. Accordingly, the notion of "God," as well as any other notional "objects" of divine science, cannot be abstracted, as such.

Article 4: On Divine Science

The famous Article 4 addresses whether divine science considers that which exists without matter and motion. The objections in this Article all voice the view that divine science cannot treat things which are without matter and motion. The objections are that: 1) God is not immediately known, but only through his effects, 2) there appears to be a type of motion associated with God, 3) the angels are also considered in this science, and they are in some kind of motion and have some type of matter, and 4) theology does treat aspects of the created order which are material and in motion. It may be noted that there is already some admixture of elements in the themes of the objections, for a concern with angels is more properly in the domain of *sacra doctrina*, as envisaged by Aquinas, and the final use of the term *theologia* also indicates a partial shift or a mixing of focus from pure metaphysics to the realm of Christian theology.

It is in the response of this Article that Aquinas not only proposes that there is a rational science (first philosophy, metaphysics, or divine science) which treats that which exists without matter and motion, but also tries to distinguish this from sacred theology. With regard to the rational science of metaphysics, Aquinas here gives a long list of its various types of objects. He does not specify here that the object of metaphysics is "being," but begins by saying that any particular science considers a subject-genus, and that each science must investigate the principles of that genus, since science is perfected only through the knowledge of principles.[105] Divine science, for Aquinas, is properly concerned with *the principles* of being and is not, in fact, properly concerned with *the principle* of being, as God. This is so because the

---

[104] When Aquinas refers to "the third act of reason" in his "Prologue" to the *In Post. Anal.*, he simply states that this involves advancing from one thing to another in such a way that through that which is known, knowledge of what was unknown is attained. But Aquinas never asserts that there is a knowledge *quid est* in divine science or metaphysics.

[105] Cf. Aristotle, *Physics*, I.

highest causes include, for Aquinas, the celestial bodies and the angels, in addition to God. Now the way in which rational divine science can study these divine things is only by way of their effects, and divine science then leads to a consideration of "being as being" ("ens in quantum est ens").

> Est autem alius modus cognoscendi huiusmodi res, non secundum quod per effectus manifestantur, sed secundum quod ipsae se ipsas manifestant. Et hunc modum ponit Apostolus 1 Cor. 2: 'Quae sunt dei, nemo novit nisi spiritus dei. Nos autem non spiritum huius mundi accepimus, sed spiritum qui a deo est, ut sciamus.' Et ibidem, 'Nobis autem revelavit deus per spiritum suum.' Et per hunc modum tractantur res divinae, secundum quod in se ipsis subsistunt et non solum prout sunt rerum principia.[106]

There are several important points of note here. First of all the form of the distinction is an appeal to authority, specifically the authority of Sacred Scripture. Secondly, the mode of "knowledge" proposed in this appeal to Scripture is utterly mysterious, and there is, of course, the hermeneutical problem of what "Spirit" and "knowledge" would mean originally in 1 Cor. and how Aquinas interprets these terms. In the biblical citation itself, there is a dialectical tension: only the Spirit of God "knows" God (infinite) *but* this Spirit is received by human beings (finite) with the result of a sort of supernatural knowledge or understanding (paradox). The further and very difficult point is Aquinas' insistence here that the action of the infinite Spirit in the finite realm yields a sort of immediate knowledge of divine things for finite consciousness, for divine things are then known "secundum quod in se ipsis subsistunt" ("as they are in themselves, subsisting in themselves"). This would include here a knowledge of God as he is In-Himself, but it would seem more accurate to say that even in faithed-sacred theology, God is not known as he is In-Himself; there is only a partial increase over natural knowledge of God, so that God is known at least somewhat "more" - though not "quantitatively" - than he is known by mere natural knowledge. But in comparison with the infinity that is God, this knowledge by faith and theology is certainly not knowledge of God *per se*.

The central point of interest here is the dialectical play between the natural and supernatural orders of knowledge. The proposed, more immediate knowledge of God through the Spirit of God does not eliminate knowledge of God through his effects, for it is said that even with divine revelation through

---

[106] Aquinas, *Expositio Super Librum Boethii De Trinitate*, q. 5, a. 4, resp. (pp. 194-195). There is, however, another way of knowing such [divine] things, not according as their effects manifest them, but as the very [divine] things manifest themselves. The Apostle mentions this way in 1 Cor. 2: 'So the things also that are of God no man knows, but the Spirit of God. Now we have received not the spirit of this world, but the Spirit that is of God, that we may have knowledge.' And again, 'But to us God has revealed them through his Spirit.' And in this way divine things are treated according as they subsist in themselves and not only insofar as they are principles of things.

the action of the Spirit divine things are known "non solum prout sunt rerum principia" ("not only insofar as they are principles of things"). So, even in sacred theology, the two modes work together, at least in this conclusion of Aquinas' statement, even though the introductory sentence in this text says "*non* secundum quod per effectus manifestantur, *sed* secundum quod ipsae se ipsas manifestant" ("*not* according as [divine things] are manifested by their effects, *but* according as they themselves reveal themselves") [emphasis added]. There is a very difficult tension here. Aquinas' "theological epistemology" is far more illuminationist and Neoplatonic than his "philosophical epistemology" of human cognition. What he proposes here is a mode of knowledge by means of revelation which seems to completely circumscribe the natural order of sensation and the reasoning from effects to causes, while at the same time the potentiality or ability of the mind to be so illuminated is itself part of the "natural order." But this "illuminationist" theory of revelation is the key problem, for Aquinas repeatedly treats such immediate revelation as if it could have independent "content," not based on abstraction from the sensible domain or interpretation of experience.

There is also an underlying analogy at work between the natural and supernatural orders. In the natural order it is the participationist-transcendental structure of the "light" of the "agent intellect" which grounds the possibility of knowledge of the first principles, which grounds the possibility of all judgements, and thus it is the natural "light" of the "agent intellect" which grounds any judgements based on negation-separation, composition or division, and causal reasoning. Natural knowledge of metaphysical "objects" is possible because of the transcendental structure of the knower. Likewise in the supernatural order, the naturally given participationist-transcendental structure of the "agent intellect" is open to the *lumen fidei* which is received because of the (appropriated) action of the Holy Spirit and which grounds the possibility of all "judgements" of divine things (here "judgement" in the sense of "assent" to a reality or truth, or negation of such assent), which *then* grounds the possibility of knowledge of the articles of faith, which then grounds the possibility of all further faithed-judgements based on negation-separation, composition or division, or causal reasoning. Supernatural knowledge of The Truth of faith is possible because of the naturally given transcendental structure of the human person, which is modified or expanded somehow by the *lumen fidei* to form a "new," supernaturally transcendental structure.

In natural intellectual apprehension, it is the light of the agent intellect which illumines the object and makes it intentionally present, and it is the light of the agent intellect which makes judgement possible through the "prior" grasp of primary notions and the first principles. In natural acts of judgement, it is the light of the agent intellect which gives the object intentional existence. One may legitimately understand Aquinas to mean that in the second operation of the intellect, it is the very light of the agent intellect itself which functions as the "intentional copula,"[107] which is then either affirmed as a "copula" or denied. The "intentional copula" on the natural level may be regarded as the mental "est" which is provided by the light of the agent intellect in the second operation of the intellect. This "intentional copula" gathers the "many" into an affirmative proposition and what the intellect then knows is the one "est" as relation, for the intellect cannot focus on the multiple, but only on the singular. In negative judgement, this "est" is negated. The possibility for negative judgements proper to metaphysics would be the "implicit" knowledge of immaterial being which "exists" "in" the "agent intellect." This is not an idealism, for the structure of the agent intellect and the primary *notio entis* place the agent intellect and the primary *notio entis* in the order of the real. The light of the agent intellect then grounds the third act of causal reasoning precisely as an implicit grasp of causality, and thus also an implicit grasp of analogy and participation.

The supernatural *lumen fidei* may also be understood to function as the "intentional copula" with regard to the assent to the First Truth of Faith, and the articles of faith. The constant process of dialectical negation in finite theology is then *necessary* because what can be assented to in faithed-judgement is beyond essential grasp. The *lumen fidei* gathers the "many" articulated truths of faith into "one," and guides all "judgements" which are made on the articles of faith more by way of an effective and intellectual "instinct" for the divine than by way of full conceptual clarity. The *lumen fidei* brings a new proportionality of finite to Infinite Consciousness.

On the natural level, the active potentiality of the light of the agent intellect may be understood as a "pre-grasp" or "Vorgriff" in the sense of "reaching for but never completely grasping" Being Itself.[108] On the natural level, this active potentiality never comes to a full grasp of Being Itself; rather, the light of the agent intellect serves as the "horizon" of human knowledge, and what lies beyond this "horizon" cannot be "seen" as it lies beyond the range, or power, or "intensity of esse" (as the ability to illuminate with intentional existence) of the agent intellect. In this sense, the "horizon" functions as a limiting principle. In natural negative judgements proper to metaphysics, this "horizon as limit" is itself negated as the ultimate limit for being. So too, *ex convenientia* on the supernatural level, the *lumen fidei* - which is a received, finite participation - never comes to a full grasp of The Truth of faith, but, rather, sets up a continuing dialectical spiral, in which anything that can be fully grasped conceptually is negated, i.e., is realized not to adequately

---

[107] Cf. Aquinas, *Quodlib*. 9, a. 3, resp., where he holds that "esse" is said in two ways: "uno modo secundum quod est copula verbalis significans compositionem ... . Alio mode esse dicitur actus entis."

[108] Cf. A. Tallon, "Spirit, Matter, Becoming: Karl Rahner's 'Spirit in the World (Geist in Welt),'" *The Modern Schoolman* 48 (1971), 151-165.

contain the mystery of the revealed and concealed God. The *lumen fidei* is finite - at least as received by a finite subject - and thus serves as a limited and limiting horizon. That which is beyond this horizon cannot be adequately "illuminated" for conceptual grasp, and anything which can be adequately "illuminated" is negated, i.e., judged to be inadequate.

Further, even as the natural light of the agent intellect cannot reflect upon itself, simply in and through itself, but is only revealed to itself when it comes to know other things, so too the supernatural *lumen fidei* cannot reflect on itself in and of itself, but only in and through actual operations of assent to The Truth of faith. In a more "realistic" theological epistemology, this act of assent to The Truth of faith is not immediate, but "in and beyond" the interpretation of experience brought about by the changed intentionality made possible by the *lumen fidei*. But, again, the point of the analogy here between the *lumen naturale* and the *lumen fidei* is that neither light comes to an immediate reflection on itself. Both "lights" can only reflect on themselves through operations. Now, on the natural level, there is a sense in which the end-point of natural metaphysics is the end-point of philosophical anthropology. This is so precisely because metaphysics, as an operation of the *lumen naturale*, and as the absolute limit of natural knowledge, must be engaged in order that the *lumen naturale* can comprehensively consider what it itself is. And this *lumen naturale* cannot consider itself directly, but only in and through operations. So too, by analogy, *ex convenientia*, there is a sense in which the end-point of faithed-theological reflection-assent to The Trinitarian Truth of faith is the end-point of theological anthropology. In other words, it is the concern of theological anthropology to present an integrated understanding of the nature of the human person as open to and as effected by the *lumen fidei*. But this *lumen fidei* cannot reflect upon itself, and so its nature can only be known in and through its operations, most particularly, in its assent to the most sublime and the highest mystery of faith, namely, the Trinity. If one approaches the exploration of the *lumen fidei* in this manner, then one's statements are much more apt to be qualified and cautious regarding the possible extent of theological knowledge. Unfortunately, Aquinas himself never actually makes it clear that the end-point in philosophical anthropology is in a sense simultaneous with the end-point in metaphysics. But it is the basis for this position in Aquinas which has been exploited so admirably in the "transcendental phenomenology" of Lonergan. An additionally unfortunate point is that Aquinas usually does not practice a reflection on the nature of the *lumen fidei* by examining what it actually accomplishes in the human subject *in via* in the ultimate test-case of faithed-knowledge of the Trinity. What Aquinas, unfortunately, is more prone to do is to proceed in a "deductive" manner, by arguing from the nature of the *lumen gloriae* to what the nature of the *lumen fidei* and divine revelation in this life should be. The result of this is that he constructs a theological anthropology which for all practical purposes portrays human subjects as if they were much more "angelic" substances, whose mode of knowledge is immediate and not encumbered by the abstraction of forms and the "interpretation of experience." Nevertheless, based on Aquinas' perhaps too infrequent cautionary notes about the possible limits of theological knowledge, and based on more Aristotelian elements in Aquinas' philosophical epistemology, one can argue that there is a legitimate interpretation of Aquinas which holds that the way to come to knowledge of the nature of the *lumen fidei* is to examine its actual operations in this life. Of course, any such investigation is more difficult than philosophical epistemology.

In the immediately following paragraph of his *Expositio*, Aquinas shifts his emphasis in the distinction slightly. Now it is not said that sacred theology treats divine things immediately, with a knowledge of them as they subsist in themselves, but merely that sacred theology considers divine things "propter se ipsas" ("for their own sakes"):

> Sic ergo theologia sive scientia divina est duplex. Una, in qua considerantur res divinae non tamquam subiectum scientiae, sed tamquam principia subiecti, et talis est theologia, quam philosophi prosequuntur, quae alio nomine metaphysica dicitur. Alia vero, quae ipsas res divinas considerat propter se ipsas ut subiectum scientiae, et haec est theologia, quae in sacra scriptura traditur.[109]

The emphasis here is milder, for it is one thing to know divine things as they are in themselves, subsisting in themselves, and it is quite another thing to consider divine things in a contemplative manner which is not full knowledge but which regards the divine, as revealed, as the highest good, worthy of consideration for its own sake.

Now, Aquinas is in the midst of a distinction between metaphysics and sacred theology, and all of the remaining articles of his *Expositio* will focus on the particular nature of metaphysics, as a science treating that which exists without matter and motion. One may wonder, therefore, if Aquinas will somehow hold that sacred theology, as distinguished from metaphysics, actually does treat that which exists in matter and motion, in some sense of the term. If Aquinas holds that both metaphysics and sacred theology treat things that exist without matter and motion, then all the prohibitions which Aquinas lists for metaphysics, regarding the abandonment of imagination and

---

[109] Aquinas, *Expositio Super Librum Boethii De Trinitate*, q. 5, a. 4, resp. (p. 195). From this, therefore, theology or divine science is twofold. There is one in which divine things are treated not as the subject of the science, but as the principles of the subject, and this type is the theology which is pursued by the philosophers and which by another name is called metaphysics. Another type of theology is that which considers divine things for their own sakes as the subject of the science, and this is the type of theology which is taught in Sacred Scripture.

the possibility of beholding the divine Form, would also seem to apply in some way, problematically, to sacred theology.

Now what Aquinas does in fact do in this Article is to immediately say that both metaphysics and sacred theology treat what exists apart from matter and motion: "*Utraque* autem est de his quae sunt separata a materia et motu secundum esse, sed diversimode [emphasis added]."[110] The question is, then, what this "diversimode" could mean and if it will have any impact on the role of imagination in sacred theology, or the possibility of beholding the divine Form in sacred theology.

Aquinas proposes two modes in which a thing may exist separate from matter and motion. The first is an absolute way, as is the case with God and the angels, who are said never to exist in matter and motion. The second is a possibly mixed way, as is the case with realities considered by metaphysics such as "being" (i.e., "ens"), "substance," "potency," and "act," which can exist apart from matter and motion, but can also exist in matter and motion.

Aquinas then tries to distinguish metaphysics from sacred theology by saying that metaphysics can only investigate things such as "being" ("ens"), "substance," "potency," and "act," which are in a possibly mixed condition of separation from matter and motion, as the proper *subjects* of metaphysics, while metaphysics can also treat God and the angels, indirectly, as the principles of its proper subjects. However,

> Theologia vero sacrae scripturae tractat de separatis primo modo sicut de subiectis, quamvis in ea tractentur aliqua quae sunt in materia et motu, secundum quod requirit rerum divinarum manifestatio.[111]

Aquinas, as has been seen, has earlier denied in this Article that metaphysics can actually treat "God" as its "subject." For him, metaphysics is limited to treating God as the "principle" of its "proper subjects." He then states that the theology of Sacred Scripture can treat separate things, i.e., God, the angels, etc., as its "subjects." Here it is as if metaphysics would only be interested in God for the sake of the "subjects" which it really seeks to treat. But this is in a way an artificial limitation on metaphysics. While metaphysics as such can certainly not treat God as revealed, it can be interested in God In-Himself, for His own sake, and not simply as the Principle of other subjects. Here Aquinas' distinction between metaphysics and sacred theology is strained and not completely satisfactory. It is possible for both metaphysics

---

[110] Ibid. *Both* are concerned with those things that are separate from matter and motion according to their being, but in a different way [emphasis added].

[111] Ibid. The theology of Sacred Scripture treats separate things in the first sense as its subjects, though some things which exist in matter and motion are also treated by it, insofar as this is needed for the manifestation of divine things.

and sacred theology to treat things that can exist in matter and motion only in order to reach a greater manifestation of the Absolute which is God.

As to the more basic problem posed in this text, it remains the case that Aquinas proposes that the ultimate subject of sacred theology is something that exists beyond matter and motion, and thus his later prohibitions in the *Expositio* regarding the imagination and the possibility of beholding the divine Form would seem to apply equally to metaphysics and to sacred theology. This poses a particular problem for sacred theology, in a manner never fully clarified by Aquinas, in that biblical revelation is in terms of experience and symbols, which precisely appeal to the imagination.

Question 6: The Methods of the Speculative Sciences

Question 6, the final Question in Aquinas' unfinished *Expositio*, consists of four articles: 1) whether the mode of procedure in natural science is reason, in mathematics is learning, and in divine science is intellect, 2) whether the imagination should be abandoned in divine science, 3) whether the human intellect can behold the divine form itself, and 4) whether the human intellect can behold the divine form by means of some speculative science. Several initial points may be noted. The term used for the mode of procedure in natural science (i.e., natural philosophy) is "rationabiliter," meaning "reasonably" or "according to reason." The term used for mathematics (i.e., for the medievals and Aquinas, "arithmetic and Eucledian geometry") is "disciplinabiliter," meaning "by way of disciplined study or learning." The term used with regard to divine science (i.e., metaphysics) is "intellectualiter," meaning "intellectually," or "by way of the intellect." The second initial point that should be noted is that the abandonment of the imagination is first stated only with regard to divine science as metaphysics, and not with regard to sacred theology as such. But based on the text of Boethius and the progression of Aquinas' thought in the *Expositio*, it is clear that Aquinas was constructing an argument for some sort of negation of the imagination in sacred theology.

Article 1: Reason, Disciplined Learning, and Intellect

This is an important Article because it involves making distinctions among the modes of inquiry which can be termed "reason," "disciplined learning," and "intellect." The distinction is particularly interesting with regard to the idea that metaphysics and, perhaps, sacred theology do not so much proceed by way of "reason," as by "intellect," possibly with "intellectualiter" even referring to "understanding."

In this Article 1, Aquinas describes the "rational" procedure of reason used in natural philosophy as being an application of logic, but this also belongs to mathematics and metaphysics. And so the uniquely rational procedure proper to metaphysics cannot be logic, simply as such. Aquinas then proposes in his response that there are two other ways in which a procedure can be named a "rational" one, and the first is on the basis of the end of the procedure. Now, the initial text in the response of Article 1 in which Aquinas makes this distinction has a particular problem in the Decker edition. The problem, as will be seen, is that there is a phrase in the response which Decker presents as "probatio rationabilis," which arguably should read "probabiles rationes." The difference is important for making sense of the text, and one should recall that in the shorthand of Aquinas, "probatio rationabilis" and "probabiles rationes" would be very similar. Now, the section of the response in which Aquinas makes the distinction of the other manner of calling a procedure "rational," in Decker's edition of the text, is as follows:

> Alio modo dicitur processus rationalis ex termino in quo sistitur procedendo. Ultimus enim terminus, ad quem rationis inquisitio perducere debet, est intellectus principiorum, in quae resolvendo iudicamus; quod quidem quando fit non dicitur processus vel *probatio rationabilis*, sed demonstrativa [emphasis added].[112]

As it stands, the text is difficult to interpret. Aquinas is not talking here about "scientia" as such, but more of a rational process of understanding principles. Nevertheless, the example he gives is on the level of "scientia," i.e., the demonstration of truths. Further, the attempted distinction between "probatio rationabilis" and "demonstrativa" is impossible, as normally they mean the same thing for Aquinas.

The present author would like to propose that there is some corruption in the manuscript evidence leading to the critical edition of this text by Decker, and a corresponding error in the translations, e.g., by Maurer. If one reads the immediately following lines in the response by Aquinas, one finds reference to "probabiles rationes" and then a discussion of how these differ from the scientific method:

> Quandoque autem inquisitio rationis non potest usque ad praedictum terminum perduci, sed sistitur in ipsa inquisitione, quando scilicet inquirenti adhuc manet via ad utrumlibet; et hoc contingit, quando per *probabiles rationes* proceditur, quae natae sunt facere opinionem vel fidem, non

---

[112] Ibid., q. 6, a. 1, resp. (p. 205). In a second way a method is called rational because of the end in which the thinking process is terminated. The ultimate end that rational inquiry ought to reach is the understanding of principles, in which we reach resolution in judgements. And when this takes place it is not called a rational procedure or *proof* but a demonstration [emphasis added].

scientiam. Et sic rationabilis processus dividitur contra demonstrativum [emphasis added].[113]

Accordingly, in the present author's judgement the initial text of the response could read "per probabiles rationes" rather than "vel probatio rationabilis." This is then in continuity with what follows immediately. Thus the text in question would read:

> Alio modo dicitur processus rationalis ex termino in quo sistitur procedendo. Ultimus enim terminus, ad quem rationis inquisitio perducere debet, est intellectus principiorum, in quae resolvendo iudicamus; quod quidem quando fit non dicitur processus *per* proba*biles* ratio*nes*, sed demonstrati*o* [changes indicated in italics].[114]

At least this reading solves the initial problem of an impossible distinction between a "rational proof" and a "rational demonstration." The point of interest then is that a procedure can be rational even when it only provides probable, or one might say, *ex convenientia* "arguments," and this is obviously of importance in the Trinitarian project in which Aquinas was engaged in this *Expositio*, because there is no rational demonstration of the Trinitarian mystery, but only *ex convenientia* "arguments" aiding faith.

The third procedure which Aquinas terms "rational" in this response is also applicable to the problem of theological understanding of the Trinitarian mystery:

> Tertio modo dicitur aliquis processus rationalis a potentia rationali, in quantum scilicet in procedendo sequimur proprium modum animae rationalis in cognoscendo, et sic rationabilis processus est proprius scientiae naturalis.[115]

---

[113] Ibid. However, sometimes rational inquiry cannot arrive at the ultimate end, but stops in the course of the investigation itself, namely, when the process of inquiry can pursue several possible paths, and this happens when the procedure is by means of *probable reasons*, which form opinion or faith, but not science. And in this way the rational process of probable reasons is distinguished from demonstration [emphasis added].

[114] In a second way a method is called rational because of the end in which the thinking process is terminated. The ultimate end that rational inquiry ought to reach is the understanding of principles, in which we reach resolution in judgements. And when this takes place it is not called a rational procedure *by means of probable reasons*, but a *demonstration* [changes indicated in italics. Decker notes (p. 205) that there is some manuscript evidence for the last word as "demonstratio" and some for "rationalis" rather than "rationabilis," but he cites no evidence for "per" rather than "vel," and none for "rationes." Further analysis of the manuscript evidence would be needed before the present hypothetical corrections could be accepted].

[115] Aquinas, *Expositio Super Librum Boethii De Trinitate* (p. 206). In a third way, a procedure is called rational from the rational power, namely inasmuch as in the procedure we follow the proper mode of the rational soul in knowing, and in this sense the rational process is proper to natural science.

What Aquinas then specifies here is that the manner proper to the rational soul in knowing is that it receives from sensible things knowledge of intelligible things, and it moves from knowledge of one thing to knowledge of another. Now, this is clearly the case in natural science (philosophy), and one can at least argue that it is also the case in sacred theology: the "science" of theology, considered as a rational process of understanding, begins in the faithed-interpretation of sensible data in experience, and this "science" is rational in the sense that it follows a procedure proper to the rational soul in knowing. A procedure can be rational and "scientific" here without being demonstrative, although the scientific ideal is still demonstration.

There is some strange argumentation in the distinction between the procedure for mathematics and that for divine science, and one may anticipate that Aquinas would use different distinctions for sacred theology. In this first Article, it is argued that mathematics is more certain than natural philosophy or metaphysics, because it abstracts from matter and motion, on the one hand, and because the objects of metaphysics are further removed from sensible things, and therefore less certainly known, on the other.

The third section of the response in this Article is of particular interest because it addresses a procedure of rationality which moves "intellectualiter" in divine science:

> Ad tertiam quaestionem dicendum quod sicut rationabiliter procedere attribuitur naturali philosophiae, eo quod in ipsa maxime observatur modus rationis, ita intellectualiter procedere attribuitur divinae scientiae, eo quod in ipsa maxime observatur modus intellectus.[116]

What Aquinas seems to indicate here is that the intellectual mode of divine science, as metaphysics, surpasses the modes of reason and intellect, in that the "objects" of metaphysics are not demonstrated by reason, but shown, in some way, to be presupposed by reason. And, further, the highest causes intellectually considered by metaphysics are not fully understood, as they are in-themselves as principles, but only understood by a process of reasoning from their effects to some knowledge of them as principles. The usually overlooked point in this text of Aquinas is that there is an intellectual process of inquiry, as divine science, which does not conceptually grasp its objects, and yet it is supremely intellectual, in that it is a point of self-awareness on

---

[116] Ibid. (pp. 210-211). To the third question it is to be said that even as a rational procedure is attributed to natural philosophy, in that it is observed to be maximally in the mode of reason, so too a procedure which is intellectual is attributed to divine science, in that is is observed to maximally follow the mode of the intellect.

[One has a problem of interpretation and translation here, for "intellectus" can signify "intellect" or "understanding" with some important differences in meaning. In the present text "modus intellectus" means "mode of the intellect" rather than "mode of understanding," as is clear from the parrallel stucture and context.]

the part of intellect that it has reached its frontiers. One can only surmise that Aquinas' distinctions here were preparing the way for his unfinished conclusion to his *Expositio* of the *De Trinitate*, in which he would eventually turn to a treatment of the Trinity in an intellectual mode of sacred theology, with a stress on the incomprehensibility of the Trinitarian Mystery, and the supreme "intellectuality" of theology in recognizing this. The point here is that Aquinas is, in the text, distinguishing the processes of "reason" from those that are more eminently "intellectual":

> Differt autem ratio ab intellectu, sicut multitudo ab unitate. Unde dicit Boethius in IV De consolatione quod similiter se habent ratio ad intellectum et tempus ad aeternitatem et circulus ad centrum. Est enim rationis proprium circa multa diffundi et ex eis unam simplicem cognitionem colligere. Unde Dionysius dicit 7 c. De divinis nominibus quod animae secundum hoc habent rationalitatem quod diffusive circueunt existentium veritatem, et in hoc deficiunt ab angelis; sed in quantum convolvunt multa ad unum, quodam modo angelis aequantur. Intellectus autem e converso per prius unam et simplicem veritatem considerat et in illa totius multitudinis cognitionem capit, sicut deus intelligendo suam essentiam omnia cognoscit. Unde Dionysius ibidem dicit quod angelicae mentes habent intellectualitatem, in quantum 'uniformiter intelligibilia divinorum intelligunt.'[117]

This is a difficult text. But it is of great value to see what Aquinas means and implies about the nature of sacred theology as an intellectual process. The first point to note is that Aquinas is definitely distinguishing "reason" and "intellect," and yet these are not fully distinct powers of the soul; they are simply distinct acts of what is at root the same power. The distinction is that it is the proper act of reason to advance from the knowledge of one thing which is known to knowledge of another thing which was not previously known; while the proper act of intellect is to apprehend intelligible truth simply, or in one act in which the "totality" of the intelligible truth is grasped. This distinction is essentially the same one Aquinas makes elsewhere, as can been seen, between "scientia" and "sapientia," for "scientia" involves a

---

[117] Ibid. (p. 211). Now reason differs from intellect as multitude does from unity. Hence Boethius says, in IV *De Consolatione Philosophiae* that reason is related to intellect as time to eternity and as a circle to its center. For it is distinctive of reason to disperse itself in the many things [which it considers] and then to gather together from these things one simple act of knowing. Thus Dionysius says in Chapter 7 of the *De Divinus Nominibus* that souls insofar as they have rationality are such that they approach the truths of existing things from various angles, and in this respect they are inferior to the angels, but insofar as they gather a multiplicity into unity they are in some way equal to the angels. Conversely, intellect first contemplates a truth which is one and undivided and in that truth comprehends a whole multitude, even as God, by intellectually grasping his own essence knows all things. Thus Dionysius says in the same work that angelic minds have intellectuality ["intellectualitatem", or "intellectual power"] in that 'in a unified way they intellectually grasp [here "intelligunt"] the intelligible things of divine things ["intelligibilia divinorum"].

discursive process of reasoning while "sapientia" involves more of a contemplative consideration of the highest cause as the unified notion of all truth. Reason, as discursive and as moving from one thing to another, is involved in the temporal order; while the supreme intellectual act, considered here as "intellectuality" per se, or elsewhere as "sapientia," meaning metaphysics as the consideration of the highest causes, is involved in a contemplation of the truth as such - insofar as this is possible - and is thus at least more of a participation in what is properly eternal than is "scientia." The process of reasoning is a movement, as it were, along a line which forms the circumference of a circle. By an extension of the analogy, reason tries to look at what the totality of the circle means, and tries to look at the originating center of the circle, but can only do so from a moving viewpoint, as each conceptual moment must isolate an aspect of the totality, or a point on the circumference of the circle. By contrast, the viewpoint from the center of the circle has a horizon which is 360 degrees, the totality in one view. Reason must consider many things, in a moving horizon, in the attempt to get only partial glimpses of what the totality is, while supreme intellectuality sees all the parts in one intellectual act which grasps the totality. Insofar as the human intellect approaches the grasp of the totality in a supremely intellectual act, there is a limited, and never fully attained, sense in which human intellect is equal to the angelic, and in which the human intellect participates more fully in the One Act of comprehending the totality and Itself as origin, which is the Act of God.

In Aquinas' *Expositio* one can only conclude that the way of thought he was developing, but did not finish, was to consider divine science, as metaphysics, as the fullest possible rational and natural intellectual comprehension of the totality in a unified way, and then to consider sacred theology as supremely intellectual, in a supernatural manner, insofar as it participates in a higher way in the One Intellectual Act. The point of importance here is that the emphasized nature of sacred theology is thus not one of a discursive science, but, again, a contemplative intellectuality more properly termed "sapientia," as the perfection of the intellect, and thus the termination of "reason."

In the final reply to objections in this Article, a reply to Objection 4, Aquinas makes a link between what has been proposed thus far in the Article concerning the supreme intellectuality of divine science, and the intellectuality of faith. Since this is the conclusion of the Article, one legitimately judges that it is a point of emphasis and reflects the driving motivation of the Article. This conclusion also shows that the intention of Aquinas was not simply to give an analysis of rational metaphysics, but to make the bridge to a consideration of sacred theology. In Objection 4, it was stated that theology, now meaning "sacred theology," seems particularly concerned with things of faith, while understanding, "intelligere" is the end of things of faith. Thus it is said "unless you believe, you will not understand."Accordingly, the Objection is that it would seem that a genuinely intellectual process, here in the sense of "understanding," is not the mode of procedure for sacred theology, but the end. The mode of procedure for sacred theology would seem to be simply belief, or faith. In his response to this objection, Aquinas states:

> Ad quartum dicendum quod cognitio etiam fidei maxime pertinet ad intellectum. Non enim ea rationis investigatione accipimus, sed simplici acceptione intellectus tenemus. Dicimur autem ea non intelligere, in quantum intellectus eorum plenariam cognitionem non habet; quod quidem nobis in praemium repromittitur.[118]

This is very dialectical, and technical. The truths of faith are received in an act of assent, which can be called something like an "act of understanding," in that the truths of faith, for Aquinas, are something like "principles." But, the truths of faith are never fully understood in this life.

Here again it is assumed by Aquinas that "understanding" is more intellectual than "science," and that ultimately "wisdom" is the most intellectual of acts. All three modes have knowledge, "cognitio," but in differing manners. The knowledge of faith, *cognitio fidei*, is here clearly emphasized as intellectual, but also distinguished from *scientia*, and even from *intellectus*, and is more related to "faith filled with hope for the future" than presently actualized knowledge. Thus the present text serves as a dialectical balance to other texts which insist on the scientific status of sacred theology. It is not only the case that the First Truth, as the ultimate object of faith, is not understood in the act of faith; even the articles of faith are not actually understood in the act of faith, but only anticipated with a hope which believes they will be eventually "understood" in the *lumen gloriae*.

Article 2: Imagination and Divine Science

In Article 2 Aquinas addresses the very difficult and fundamental notion of the relation of "phantasms" of experience and "imagination" to divine science and to sacred theology.[119] And he gives some further indications of what one

---

[118] Ibid., q. 6, a. 1, ad 4 (p. 213). To the fourth objection it is to be said that the knowledge which is of faith maximally pertains to the intellect. For we do not accept the things of faith through an investigation of reason; rather, we hold the things of faith simply by receiving them in an act of understanding. But we are not said to understand them, insofar as the intellect does not have full knowledge of them; for it is that, indeed, which is promised to us as our reward.

[119] It goes without saying that by "imaginatio" Aquinas means the memory of sense experience and images. A full explication of the status of "phantasms" in Aquinas' epistemology is not needed here. There is, of course, the problematic yet illuminating discussion by Rahner in his *Spirit in the World*, which focuses on a parallel text in the *Summa Theologiae*.

104 AQUINAS: THE *EXPOSITIO* OF THE *DE TRINITATE*

one may anticipate was his plan for the extension of the discussion on divine science to sacred theology. This is even indicated in the very first objection, where an indication as to the continuity of the two domains is provided, for the objection is that divine science has been most appropriately taught in the Sacred Scriptures, but these use sensible images to talk about the divine, and so such images are appropriate in divine science. Another objection is that the divine is not known immediately, but understood indirectly through the created order, by experience of the created order, and thus imagination has a role in divine science.

There is an extremely fundamental and powerful dilemma-in-tension in this Article. One may anticipate it thusly: human experience is properly in the created order of the sensibles. Human communication, and hence divine revelation, are properly in the created order of the sensibles. Further, the ultimate moment of revelation, as the Incarnate Christ, is in the created order precisely as a human being who can enter into relationships with and be experienced by others. Further, because human intellectual understanding is not fully intellectual, as the angelic and the Divine, it cannot fully abandon sensible particulars, and the end-point of sacred theology, even as practiced by Aquinas, is a second return to the biblical texts, and a reading-encounter with its images with a new intentionality that goes through the images to the ultimate mystery which cannot be imagined. But, it would seem that the imagination remains a necessary moment in sacred theology, if not even in divine science as metaphysics. So, the difficulties that this Article will face should be clear.

In his response, Aquinas immediately acknowledges the Aristotelian principle that all knowledge begins in the senses, and that this is the beginning point for the imagination. But knowledge does not always terminate in the senses, e.g., mathematics considers objects as such independent of sensible existence. But divine science treats objects such as "being," "substance," "act," and "potency" which do not have to exist in matter, as well as God, who, technically and mysteriously, does not exist *in* matter, simply as such, even in the Incarnation. Since such objects do not exist in matter and motion, they cannot be imagined as such. The problem is that the human intellect cannot reach an understanding of these objects simply in and through themselves, or in and through itself. The human intellect must proceed through the sensible realm of the created order, even if its terminus in intellectual understanding is not in that order.

Uti ergo possumus in divinis et sensu et imaginatione sicut principiis nostrae considerationis, sed non sicut terminis, ut scilicet iudicemus talia esse divina, qualia sunt quae sensus vel imaginatio apprehendit.[120]

The problem remains, however, as to the possible status of "understanding" in both divine science and sacred theology, because what is attempted to be understood is so far beyond the senses and the imagination as to have no "content" in those orders.

In his responses to the objections in this Article, Aquinas presents a very strong emphasis on the negative way, and also still insists that all knowledge begins in the senses, thus giving a more "traditional" Aristotelian theme than an immediate illumination, Neoplatonic theme. Also of note is the fact that he does not discuss the necessary return to the domain of images and biblical revelation, and could seem to give the impression that sacred theology terminates in a pure idealism of negation on the conceptual level. Each of the responses here is profound in itself and in its implications. They are confusing in their interplay, because at times they are addressed clearly to problems in sacred theology, and at other times clearly to problems in divine science, but it is not always clear what the relationships would be between a response directed to divine science and the same response directed to sacred theology.

Ad primum ergo dicendum quod sacra scriptura non proponit nobis divina sub figuris sensibilibus, ut ibi intellectus noster remaneat, sed ut ab his ad immaterialia ascendat. Unde etiam per vilium rerum figuras divina tradit, ut minor praebeatur occasio in talibus remanendi, ut dicit Dionysius in 2 c. Caelestis hierarchiae.

Ad secundum dicendum quod intellectus nostri operatio non est in praesenti statu sine phantasmate quantum ad principium cognitionis; non tamen oportet quod nostra cognitio semper ad phantasma terminetur, ut scilicet illud, quod intelligimus, iudicemus esse tale quale est illud quod phantasia apprehendit ... .

Ad quintum dicendum quod phantasma est principium nostrae cognitionis, ut ex quo incipit intellectus operatio non sicut transiens, sed sicut permanens ut quoddam fundamentum intellectualis operationis; sicut principia demonstrationis oportet manere in omni processu scientiae, cum phantasmata comparentur ad intellectum ut obiecta, in quibus inspicit omne quod inspicit vel secundum perfectam repraesentationem vel per negationem. Et ideo quando phantasmatum cognitio impeditur, oportet totaliter impediri cognitionem intellectus etiam in divinis. Patet enim quod non possumus intelligere deum esse causam corporum sive supra omnia corpora sive absque corporeitate, nisi imaginemur corpora, non tamen iudicium divinorum secundum imaginationem formatur. Et ideo quamvis

---

[120] Aquinas, *Expositio Super Librum Boethii De Trinitate*, q. 6, a. 2, resp. (p. 217). It follows that we can use both the senses and the imagination as starting points in our consideration [of divine things], but not as the terminus of our consideration, namely, as if we would judge divine things to be of the same type as those which sensation or the imagination apprehends.

imaginatio in qualibet divinorum consideratione sit necessaria secundum statum viae, numquam tamen ad eam deduci oportet in divinis.[121]

Here Aquinas does not explain the internal, interpretive principles which allow the person in faith not to terminate understanding at the level of biblical images. The *lumen fidei* or *habitus fidei* would be this principle, but the stress here is that rather than positive knowledge of God, even in the prime font of biblical revelation, the very biblical images are sensed, by faith, to be inadequate. The First Truth which is the "object" of faith remains utterly mysterious, non-imaginable. And yet, at the same time, there is a recovery of the value of the biblical images in the Response to Objection 5, although this recovery is indirect since Aquinas is only directly addressing phantasms and divine science. In an application of Aquinas' reasoning here, one can see how it is that he does not become purely idealistic in the negative movement of divine science or sacred theology. Rather than opting for purely Neoplatonic "illumination," Aquinas here recovers Aristotelian elements in his "theological epistemology." The "phantasm," or in an extended sense, the "images and symbols," are not totally negated and overcome, rather, they *remain, as a sort of starting point for intellectual activity* ("permanens ut quoddam fundamentum intellectualis operationis"). The status of this "sort of" ("quoddam") is not specified completely. But the point is that if they did

---

would judge divine things to be of the same type as those which sensation or the imagination apprehends.

[121] Ibid., q. 6, a. 2, ad. 1, 2, 5 (pp. 217-218). To the first objection it is to be said that Sacred Scripture does not present divine things to us under sensible figures so that our intellect may remain there [at that level], but that our intellect may rise from that level in ascending to immaterial things. Hence Sacred Scripture even teaches divine things through the figures of base things, in order to offer less occasion of remaining at that level, as Dionysius says in Chapter 2 of the *Celestial Hierarchy*.

To the second objection it is to be said that the operation of our intellect in its present state is not without a phantasm with regard to the beginning point of knowledge; but it does not follow, however, that our knowledge always terminates in phantasms, which would be to say that we would judge the objects of our understanding to be the same kind of objects as those which are apprehended in phantasms ... .

To the fifth objection it is to be said that a phantasm is the starting point of our knowledge, even as it is through the phantasm that the operation of the intellect begins, not as a transient [starting point, or ground for the intellect, which then passes away and is done away with], but as [a starting point, or ground] which remains permanently and is in some way still the foundation of intellectual operations, even as the principles of demonstration remain in the whole process of science, and this is so because the phantasms are related to the intellect as objects in which ["in quibus"] it sees everything that it sees, either according to a perfect representation [of the object in the phantasm] or according to a negation [of the phantasm]. And for the same reason, when knowledge of the phantasms is impeded, it follows that there is a complete impediment of intellectual knowledge even of divine things. It is clear that it is not possible for us to know that God is the cause of bodies, or transcends all bodies or is not corporeal, unless [we are able] to imagine a body, and yet, it is nonetheless not the case that our judgement of the divine is formed according to the imagination. And for the same reason, even though the imagination is necessary for all of our considerations of divine things in this life, it in no way follows that we should terminate in the imagination in the consideration of divine things.

not remain then one would be able to overcome the limit-language of biblical revelation and attain, instead, a pure conceptuality of reason, on a higher level than faith. For Aquinas, the "phantasms" remain as the objects *in which ("in quibus")* the intellect sees whatever it sees, although the phantasm as such is not what the intellect "sees." In an extended sense, not here explicated by Aquinas, the images and symbols of biblical revelation remain as those things *in which* faith reaches some understanding of the mystery of God, and there is no consciously reflective process of assimilating divine revelation apart from the images and symbols in the domain of experience, and while the images and symbols are never adequate for the full presentation and manifestation of the divine reality, they cannot be overcome completely. The status of the images and symbols is dialectical, for they cannot be dispensed with, and yet the understanding does not terminate in them as such.

Article 3: On Beholding the Divine Form

One would expect that given the emphasis of the preceding Article 2, Aquinas would insist in the next Article that the human intellect cannot "see" the Divine Form Itself. But that is not the dialectical move of Aquinas here. He will argue that there is a mode of "seeing" the Divine Form, although it is *not* a mode which is knowledge of the Essence of God. One should note that in comparison to his earlier *Commentary on the Sentences*, Question 1, Aquinas has become more qualified and cautious.

It should be noted that Aquinas is not doing pure divine science as rational metaphysics in this Article, as it includes appeals to Sacred Scripture, at least in the *Sed contra*, and there are appeals to Ps. Dionysius, whom Aquinas regarded as an authority in sacred theology rather than metaphysics as such, which dominate the approach in the *Responsio*.

The objections all follow the line of thought one would expect, given the previous Article: the human intellect is not able to behold, "inspicere," the divine Form. The Response reverses this by asserting a distinction: there are two types of knowledge, *quid est* and *an est*. In this life, the human intellect cannot attain quidditative knowledge of God, because the human intellect is naturally directed to the levels of sensible things, phantasms, images, and symbols. But these mediations, even in biblical revelation, do not suffice for quidditative knowledge of God, and in the sense that these mediations are not adequate for an expression of the Essence of God, these mediations are "inadequate."

The Response is particularly interesting in that Aquinas strongly insists on the radically "empirical" nature of revelation in human experience, using very Aristotelian themes, and yet merges this in a transformation of "Dionysian,"

Neoplatonic negativity in a way parallel to the general transformation of Ps. Dionysius begun by Aquinas' mentor, Albert the Great:

> Divinae revelationis radius ad nos pervenit secundum modum nostrum, ut Dionysius dicit. Unde quamvis per revelationem elevemur ad aliquid cognoscendum, quod alias esset nobis ignotum, non tamen ad hoc quod alio modo cognoscamus nisi per sensibilia.[122]

The actual emphasis in Ps. Dionysius is on the total inadequacy of sensible mediations of the Divine, and the immediate nature of a blinding light of superabundant intensity. In Ps. Dionysius there is not so much an "adaptation" of divine Light to the human condition, as there is a blindness induced by the absolute radiance of the Divine, i.e., by that which is "even beyond divinity." Aquinas here modifies the more radical stance of Ps. Dionysius, and domesticates the *agnosia* of such Neoplatonism, by the introduction of Aristotelian elements. But the manner of usage of Aristotelian elements in this particular text is somewhat unique. Here Aquinas is not following Albert the Great, nor repeating his own earlier stance in the *Commentary on the Sentences*, Question 1, wherein Dionysian "Light" is made into a more Aristotelian "form" as a principle of intellectual knowledge. In the present text, there are two different Aristotelian themes which dominate. First of all, Aquinas reflects his adaptation of Aristotelian "act" and "potentiality" by holding that the received actuality of divine revelation will be according to the potentiality of the human subject. Secondly, Aquinas here uses a more empirical, Aristotelian epistemology, in which all human intellectual knowledges begins in sensory data. This would again suggest the more balanced theme which the present analysis has argued is evidenced in the texts of Aquinas, i.e., that the "light" of revelation does not itself supply the "content" of revelation, but only serves as a principle for the interpretation of experience.

The ending point of Aquinas' response is not a simple assertion of knowledge of the divine Form as such, *quid est*, in this life, but only a knowledge *an est*. The conclusion of the response is not explicitly addressed to sacred theology, but moves on the level of divine science; and yet one would think that the same conclusion must be reached regarding sacred theology: God is known most properly in this life by negation, the more negations one applies to one's understanding of the *quid est* of God, the less vaguely God is understood, and the more the absolute transcendence of God is appreciated. The Form of God can be received intellectually only by God.

---

[122] Ibid., q. 6, a. 3, resp. (p. 221). The light of divine revelation comes to us adapted to our condition, as Dionysius says [*Celestial Hierarchy* 1, n. 2]. Thus although we are elevated by revelation to know something of which we would otherwise be ignorant, revelation does not elevate us to any other mode of knowledge than by way of sensible things.

Human intellect can only attain a partial increase in participation. Human intellect can never attain absolute identity with the divine Form.

Article 4: Knowledge of the Divine Form in Speculative Science

This final Article 4 of Aquinas' unfinished *Expositio* again mixes points of focus and manners of argumentation on the levels of both divine science and sacred theology, and while their relationships are not fully resolved, one can again anticipate the direction of what Aquinas was trying to develop.

The objections in this final Article 4 are both philosophical and properly theological, and all the objections assert that the divine Form should be attainable by means of a speculative science. The argumentation of Aquinas here is clearly teleological, and there is a dialectical tension at play in the relationship of this Article and the immediately preceding one. Aquinas has argued thus far that divine science, as metaphysics, is a science, and thus it must be able to engage in demonstration. But Aristotle holds that all demonstration begins with a knowledge of essence.[123] If the Essence of God cannot be known in this life, then there can be no demonstrative metaphysical treatment of The Principle of the proper objects of metaphysics. A further, more teleological objection is that the ultimate happiness of the human person is to understand the highest causes and the separate substances in an act of wisdom, and since wisdom is a speculative science,[124] it would thus seem that the speculative science of wisdom can attain some understanding of the separate substances and the divine Form. Further, if this end could not be attained, it would frustrate the innate tendency of the human person for the highest happiness, and thus some knowledge of the separate substances and the divine Form Itself must be attainable in a speculative science.

In his response, Aquinas does not address the impact of the light of faith, but confines his discussion to the natural light of the agent intellect: the speculative sciences are confined to the domain of the naturally known first principles of reason which are made known by the light of the agent intellect. These first principles are made known when the images of sense experience are actually illuminated. But, neither these first principles, nor the light of the agent intellect, nor the illuminated phantasms can carry one beyond the domain of the senses, to a quidditative knowledge of the separate substances or of God. Thus, Aquinas gives a very strong qualification here.

On the level of rational metaphysics, one cannot reason from the effects of the separate substances and God to a quidditative knowledge of the separate

---

[123] E.g., Aristotle, *Posterior Analytics*, II, 90b24; *Metaphysics*, VII, 9, 1034a31.

[124] Cf. Aristotle, *Metaphysics*, I, 1, 982a2; 2, 982a15ff; *Nicomachean Ethics*, VI, 7, 1141a16-19, b3.

On the level of rational metaphysics, one cannot reason from the effects of the separate substances and God to a quidditative knowledge of the separate substances and God, because the effects are not fully proportioned to their causes. Although not stated here by Aquinas, the same would seem to apply on the level of revelation and the light of faith.

In his reply to Objection 3, Aquinas clearly enters the domain of sacred theology. The response is to the objection that if there is not quidditiative knowledge of the separate substances and the divine Form, then the natural end of the human person, i.e., a happiness that springs from knowledge of the separate substances and the divine Form, would be frustrated. Aquinas' reply here is very interesting, both for what it says and what it does not say:

> Ad tertium dicendum quod duplex est felicitas hominis. Una imperfecta quae est in via, de qua loquitur Philosophus, et haec consistit in contemplatione substantiarum separatarum per habitum sapientiae, imperfecta tamen et tali, qualis in via est possibilis, non ut sciatur ipsarum quiditas. Alia est perfecta in patria, in qua ipse deus per essentiam videbitur et aliae substantiae separatae. Sed haec felicitas non erit per aliquam scientiam speculativam, sed per lumen gloriae.[125]

While recognizing that this is the final Article of the *Expositio*, and recognizing that the work was unfinished, it is still legitimate to pay attention to what is not said in the present text. There is no discussion of sacred theology as offering a perfect contemplation of the divine in this life, in the form of a speculative science. And the only mention of Aristotelian wisdom is by way of contrast, rather than similarity, to the perfection of Christian *sapientia* in Beatific Vision, which Aquinas here also *contrasts* to *any sort of speculative science*!

While Aquinas is very brief here, what is said is that the naturally attainable habit of wisdom in this life is imperfect, and his comment "qualis in via est possibilis" seems to indicate that this habit is attained only by a few, and this could thus lead into an argument for the appropriateness of divine revelation and the gift of wisdom, but the connection is not made. What is said here is that perfect happiness comes in a vision *through* the essence of God, "ipse deus *per* essentiam"; it is not said that there is a vision *of the essence of God*. This is still limit-discourse, and the intended referential value

---

[125] Aquinas, *Expositio Super Librum Boethii De Trinitate*, q. 6, a. 4, ad 3 (pp. 228-229). To the third objection it is to be said that the happiness of the human person is twofold. There is an imperfect happiness in this life, of which Aristotle speaks, and this consists in the contemplation of the separate substances through the habit of wisdom. But this contemplation is imperfect, for even insofar as it is possible in this life, it is not the case that with this habit of wisdom we can see the quiddities of the separate substances. The other type of happiness is the perfect happiness in heaven, in which God himself and the other separate substances will be seen through the essence of God. But this happiness will not come about through any sort of speculative science, but through the light of glory.

of the distinction cannot possibly be comprehended. The dialectical tension in Aquinas is that he wants to argue for the teleological completion of the human subject while also maintaining the infinite distance between God and the created order. The more mature Aquinas has here become more cautious in his assertions, compared with the early *Commentary on the Sentences*, which went so far as to assert a kind of immediate impression of the divine on the human subject in the light of revelation.

In the present text, Aquinas also *denies* that Beatific Vision will constitute a speculative science, because the nature of such vision is more *unlike* any "science," even the contemplative science of wisdom, than like any "science." What is not addressed by Aquinas here is the status of sacred theology in this life. But, given the structure and content of Aquinas' argumentation here, one could argue that sacred theology in this life is most properly understood as *not* being a speculative science. For if the perfection of faith and theological understanding in Beatific Vision manifests the nature of faith and theology in via, and such perfection is not properly *scientia*, then neither faith nor theological understanding is properly *scientia*. Here Aquinas is reversing his more usual *ex convenientia* argumentation.

CHAPTER FOUR

CONCLUSION

This study has sought to disclose the theological methodology and contents of Aquinas' *Expositio* of the *De Trinitate* of Boethius, with attention to these elements in the Tractate itself.

The method of this study has been one which integrated participationist, transcendental, and analogical thematics in 20th-century thomistic studies. Particularly, the method has integrated the dialectical aspects in each of these thematics with those in the others. Attention has been given to the dialectical interplays of the natural and supernatural participations of the human subject, in ways that would provide a transcendental reading of Aquinas, while retaining themes from participationist and analogical literature.

The procedure has been one of careful textual analysis and criticism, wherein the integrative and dialectical approach would benefit both reflections on theological methodology and a theology of the Trinity.

Participationist, Transcendental, and Analogical Thematics

The participationist reading of Aquinas is particularly valuable in its general insight that Aquinas actually provided a "synthesis" which can at times be called an Aristotelianism specified by Platonism, and at times a fundamental Platonism specified by Aristotelianism. However, the major 20th-century interpretations of participation in Aquinas have not explored transcendental and dialectical themes in the manner the present study has attempted.

Transcendental interpretations of Aquinas have stressed attention to the processes of human cognition in which one is engaged while attending to theological projects. The present study has shown that this authentically reflects the method and content of Aquinas, but has also illustrated that there is a dialectical structure in Aquinas' texts - and, by implication, in human consciousness - far beyond the usual concerns of "transcendental thomists."

Analyses of analogy in Aquinas have explicated the central link of analogy and participation in his philosophy and theology, but have often rejected transcendental readings. While it is the case that an understanding of participation is the foundation for an understanding of analogy, it is also the case that as soon as one is engaged in an analogical understanding of God based on an understanding of the structure of human consciousness, one is engaged in a transcendental-analogical process which is qualified at each step with dialectical elements.

The value of Aquinas' Trinitarian theology lies both in the albeit limited content it is able to achieve and, perhaps more importantly, in what is revealed about Christian consciousness and the structure of faithed-intentionality as one embarks upon the arduous path of seeking some understanding of ultimate Mystery. The theme here is an important one often overlooked even by late-20th-century thomistic scholars: even as, for Aquinas, the natural structure of the agent intellect cannot be known by the human subject directly, in- and of-itself, but only indirectly, as it is only able to reflect upon itself by means of reflecting upon its operations in coming-to-know - and thus the end-point of metaphysics is also the end-point of philosophical anthropology; so too the theologically considered structure of the human subject as "imago Dei" with a "supernaturally augmented" agent intellect, because of the "light" of divine grace and revelation, cannot be known in- and of-itself, directly, but only indirectly, as this structure is able, somehow, to reflect on its operations in "coming-to-know" the Trinitarian Mystery, and thus the end-point of Trinitarian theology is also the end-point of theological anthropology. Since Christian understanding of the Trinity is so radically a matter of faith, a reflection on what is involved in this Trinitarian-directed assent of faith may well help to ease stereotypic misunderstandings of basic Christian intentionality. It may well be that there is a more profound negativity of *agnosia* and a more profound dialectical movement of remotion in Aquinas' understanding of faith, theology, and the Trinity than even that presented by Barth. The negation in Aquinas may be even more profound precisely because he first affirms the entire domain of natural, rational knowledge and the necessity of entrance into reasoned discourse. Then he negates the adequacy of this domain, even when enlightened by faith, for an adequate understanding of God; but also recovers this domain as all the human subject can adequately undertake and thus must undertake, even though it ultimately faces negation. It may well be that this spiraling dialectic in Aquinas also offers far greater insight into the structure of human consciousness and language than is possible with Barth.

Toward Criticisms of 20th-Century Interpretations

At this juncture of history one is still too close to developments to offer a full appraisal and analysis of the multiple hermeneutical and doctrinal paradigms which have emerged in 20th-century "thomistic studies." And the procedure of the present study has been only to acknowledge these paradigms as major horizons for interpretations of Aquinas, rather than analyze them in their full, individual details. Nevertheless, some preliminary indications have been evidenced in the present study.[1]

It would seem that Fabro's[2] very global criticisms of Maréchal, Lotz, Rahner, Marc, Coreth, Brugger, Metz, and Lonergan are far too general, historically questionable, and fundamentally inaccurate. A similar judgement can be made of Maurer's[3] criticism of Rahner.

Most 20th-century interpretations of Aquinas' theological methodology seem to be far too simplistic. One can see that the more monolithic "thomism," e.g., of Garrigou-Lagrange,[4] was overcome by more careful historical studies, e.g., Congar, Preller, McCool;[5] but it is unfortuate that these better, historical studies were not considered by critics, such as Tracy,[6] who apparently judged "thomistic thought" to mean about the same thing as "decadent scholasticism."

With regard to Aquinas' method, Corbin's[7] work has been refreshing in an attempted "hegelian" reading of Aquinas, but the present study has indicated that an even more "hegelian" and dialectical analysis can be beneficial.

As far as the specifically Trinitarian theology in Aquinas' *Expositio* is concerned, the present study has thoroughly documented that, in the procedure of Aquinas, the "Trinitarian question" concerns both what theology can understand of the Trinity In-Itself and what it can understand of the structure of human cognition. It is clear that in Aquinas' procedure it is only with an adequately formulated natural epistemology that one can develop a theology of the act of faith and its "contents." Further, it is only with an adequately formulated theological anthropology that one can develop a theology of the Trinity; and it is only with an adequately formulated Trinitarian theology that one can develop a theology of the structure of human consciousness. In something of a "hegelian" and dialectical sense, insofar as the fundamental nature of the human subject is theologically considered to be "imago Dei," the Trinitarian question is also ultimately a question of theological anthropology.

Barthian paradigms in Trinitarian theology are significant influences on 20th-century Christian reflection. While it is of merit to be aware of the

---

[1]   For further discussion see our "Participated Trinitarian Relations: Dialectics of Method, Understanding, and Mystery in the Theology of St. Thomas Aquinas."
[2]   Fabro, "The Intensive Hermeneutics of Thomistic Philosophy: The Notion of Participation," p. 470, fn68.
[3]   Maurer. "Introduction," in *Thomas Aquinas: Faith, Reason and Theology*, p. x, fn9.
[4]   Garrigou-Lagrange, *De Deo Uno: Commentarium in Primam Partem S. Thomae.*
[5]   Congar, "Théologie," *Dictionnaire de Théologie Catholique*; Preller, *Divine Science and the Science of God: A Reformulation of Thomas Aquinas*; McCool, *Catholic Theology in the Nineteenth Century*; *From Unity to Pluralism.*
[6]   Tracy, *Blessed Rage for Order.*
[7]   Corbin, *Le chemin de la théologie chez Thomas d'Aquin.*

limitations of human, analogical language and cognition, a Barthian approach may rush to a conclusion that the Trinitarian mystery is utterly unintelligible, without transversing the rational domain in order to understand why this is so.

Rahner and Lonergan have unquestionably been the most influential "transcendental thomists" of the 20th century. Each undertook analyses of human cognition and Trinitarian theology. Based on what the present study has revealed, a further elaboration and development of their transcendental themes would be warranted. In contrast, the Trinitarian project of Nicolas[8] can be judged to be so general, and by design not concerned with details in historical developments, as to be valuable only as a broad introduction to themes. Another major weakness is Nicolas' tendency to objectivize metaphysical analogies in Aquinas' Trinitarian theology. As the present study has made clear, in his *Expositio*, Aquinas' lines of dialectical reasoning lead one to conclude that human discourse about the Trinity is more "contentless" than objective.

As to interpretations in the literature which have addressed the *Expositio* itself, the present study has provided a more detailed analysis than the introductory treatments by McInerny, Maurer, and Klünker and evidenced more qualified meanings and dialectical structures - surface and deep - than Elders.[9]

A Summary of Dialectical Themes in the Expositio

Several points of dialectical importance have emerged in the present analysis of the *Expositio*. As is the case in the *Commentary on the Sentences*, Aquinas actually has a process of internal negation in the progression of his arguments. For example, on the one hand, he presents the following positions:

> [1] Naturalis mentis humanae intuitus pondere corruptibilis corporis aggravatus in prima veritatis luce, ex qua omnia sunt facile cognoscibilia, defigi non potest.[10]

Here, sensory experience impedes the purity of a possibly "direct" Neoplatonic illumination. And there is no dialectical qualification.

---

8 Nicolas, *Synthèse dogmatique: de la Trinité à la Trinité*.

9 McInerny, *Boethius and Aquinas*; Maurer, "Introduction," in *Thomas Aquinas: Faith, Reason and Theology*; Klünker, "Einführung," in *Thomas von Aquin: Über die Trinität*; Elders, *Faith and Science: An Introduction to St. Thomas' 'Expositio in Boethii De Trinitate.'*

10 Aquinas, *Expositio Super Librum Boethii De Trinitate*, "Prologue." The natural intuition of the human mind, burdened as it is by weight of a corruptible body, is not able to fix its gaze in the first light of truth, in which all things are easily knowable.

[2] Sicut ergo naturalis cognitionis principium est creaturae notitia a sensu accepta, ita cognitionis desuper datae principium est primae veritatis notitia per fidem infusa. Et hinc est quod diverso ordine hinc inde proceditur. Philosophi enim, qui naturalis cognitionis ordinem sequuntur, praeordinant scientiam de creaturis scientiae divinae, scilicet naturalem metaphysicae. Sed apud theologos proceditur e converso, ut creatoris consideratio considerationem praeveniat creaturae.[11]

Here, there is a direct "infusion" or "illumination" of the knowledge of the First Truth, and the highly problematic proposal that the theologian could consider God *prior* to creatures. And here there is also no dialectical qualification.

[3] Ad quartum dicendum quod lumen intelligibile, ubi est purum sicut in angelis, sine difficultate omnia cognita naturaliter demonstrat, ita quod in eis est omnia naturalia cognoscere. In nobis autem lumen intelligibile est obumbratum per coniunctionem ad corpus et ad vires corporeas, et ex hoc impeditur, ut non libere possit veritatem etiam naturaliter cognoscibilem inspicere, secundum illud Sap. 10 (9,15): 'Corpus quod corrumpitur' etc. Et exinde est quod non est omnino in nobis veritatem cognoscere, scilicet propter impedimenta. Sed unusquisque magis vel minus habet hoc in potestate, secundum quod lumen intelligibile est in ipso purius.[12]

Here again, the Neoplatonic view of the body is as a hindrance to knowledge, rather than as a helpful and necessary medium for sensory experience. It is as if, problematically, natural human knowledge would be more perfect if not mediated through the body. And here there is also no dialectical qualification, by means of Aristotelian thought, to this Neoplatonic epistemology.

[4] Et secundum hoc de divinis duplex scientia habetur. Una secundum modum nostrum, qui sensibilium principia accipit ad notificandum divina, et sic de divinis philosophi scientiam tradiderunt, philosophiam primam scientiam divinam dicentes. Alia secundum modum ipsorum divinorum, ut

---

[11]   Ibid. Therefore, as the principle of natural cognition is the notion of created things, obtained by means of the senses, so too the principle of the cognition of those things which are beyond the natural order is the notion of the first truth, which is infused by means of faith. As a result there is a different order of procedure. Philosophers, who follow the way of natural cognition, order the science of creatures as prior to the science of divine things, that is, metaphysics. But theologians proceed in the reverse order, so that the consideration of the Creator comes prior to the consideration of creatures.

[12]   Ibid., q. 1, a. 1, ad 4. To the fourth objection it is to be said that intelligible light, where it is pure as in the case of the angels, has demonstrative knowledge [makes evident] without difficulty all things which are naturally known, so that in them [the angels] there is a knowing of all objects which are naturally known. In us, however, this intelligible light is obscure, being weighed down by its conjunction with the body and with corporeal powers, and on this account it is hindered and it is not able to freely behold that truth which is naturally knowable, as is said in Wisdom 10 [9,15]: 'For the corruptible body,' etc. [is a load upon the soul; and the earthly habitation burdens the thoughtful mind]. From this it follows that on account of the impediment

ipsa divina secundum se ipsa capiantur, quae quidem perfecte in statu viae
nobis est impossibilis, sed fit nobis in statu viae *quaedam* illius cognitionis
participatio et assimilatio ad cognitionem divinam, *in quantum* per fidem
nobis infusam inhaeremus ipsi primae veritati propter se ipsam [emphasis
added].[13]

Here again, theology proceeds by way of an infusion of faith, rather than
through sensible realities, although the qualification of Aquinas here is that
this immediate infusion *in via* remains imperfect.

[5] Lumen autem fidei, quod est *quasi quaedam* sigillatio primae veritatis
in mente, non potest fallere, sicut nec deus potest decipi vel mentiri, unde
hoc lumen sufficit ad iudicandum [emphasis added].[14]

Here, the relatively weak impression of God given by the light of faith is held
to be sufficient in and of itself for making judgements on matters of faith, and
one can get the impression that this light suffices for the "content" of faith,
but the manner of attaining the "content" for such judgement is not
explicated. What Aquinas stresses here is the "impression of the first truth
upon the mind" by the light of faith itself, rather than the interpretation, and
judgement, of sensory experience in a way that would lead to a vague, dark,
and veiled knowledge of the First Truth. But, insofar as the light of faith is *as
it were* only *a kind of* impression of the First Truth, then this light only, *as it
were, kind of* suffices for making judgements on matters of faith.

In contrast to the above, sometimes - though usually not - dialectically
qualified, positions, in this *Expositio* Aquinas has also argued the following:

[1] Ad sextum dicendum quod deus honoratur silentio, non quod nihil de
ipso dicatur vel inquiratur, sed quia quidquid de ipso dicamus vel
inquiramus, intelligimus nos ab eius comprehensione defecisse, unde dicitur

---

[of the body], we do not know all truth. But each one possesses more or less the power [to know
the truth] according to the purity of intelligible light which is in him.

[13] Ibid., q. 2, a. 2, resp. And from this it follows that there is a twofold science of the divine.
One is according to our mode, for which sensible things serve as principles for coming to
knowledge of divine things, and this is the divine science which the philosophers handed down,
calling first philosophy divine science. The other mode [of a science of the divine] is according
to the divine things themselves, as they are attained [understood, or known, "capiantur"] in
themselves, which is a mode that is, indeed, impossible for us to attain perfectly in this life; but
there is for us in this life *something like* that mode of cognition, by means of a participation in
and assimilation to a cognition of the divine, *inasmuch as* through the faith which is infused in us
we adhere to the First Truth itself, on account of itself [emphasis added].

[14] Ibid., q. 3, a. 1, ad 4. The light of faith, which is, *as it were, a kind of* impression of the
first truth upon the mind, cannot deceive, any more than God can be deceived or lie, and
therefore this light suffices for making judgement [emphasis added].

Eccli. 43(32), 'Glorificantes dominum quantumcumque potueritis, supervalebit adhuc.'[15]

This stresses the remaining *agnosia* in faith.

[2] Ad septimum dicendum quod cum deus in infinitum a creatura distet, nulla creatura movetur in deum, ut ipsi adaequetur vel recipiendo ab ipso vel cognoscendo ipsum. Hoc ergo, quod in infinitum a creatura distat, non est terminus motus creaturae. Sed quaelibet creatura movetur ad hoc quod deo assimiletur plus et plus *quantum potest*. Et sic etiam humana mens semper debet moveri ad cognoscendum de deo plus et plus secundum modum suum. Unde dicit Hilarius, 'Qui pie infinita persequitur, etsi non contingat aliquando, tamen semper proficiet prodeundo' [emphasis added].[16]

This qualifies all statements about the possible immediacy of divine revelation and the possible teleological fulfillment, as proposed by Aquinas, of the human person. Here the implication is that the human person *never* attains God.

[3] Divinae revelationis radius ad nos pervenit secundum modum nostrum, ut Dionysius dicit. Unde quamvis per revelationem elevemur ad *aliquid* cognoscendum, quod alias esset nobis ignotum, *non tamen ad hoc quod alio modo cognoscamus nisi per sensibilia* [emphasis added].[17]

This is the strongest dialectical qualification in the entire sequence of argumentation in the *Expositio*, and as it occurs at the ending of the work, it should be accorded some intended emphasis. The importance of this shift can hardly be overemphasized, and it is an aspect of Aquinas' thought ignored by practically all the classical commentators, and not recovered until mid-20th-century, existentially influenced, interpretations.

---

[15]   Ibid., q. 2, a. 1, ad 6. To the sixth objection it is to be said that God is honored by silence, but not in the sense that nothing may be said of him or no inquiries may be made of him, but simply in the sense that in whatever way we speak of God or make inquiries into God, we understand that our comprehension of God is deficient, hence it is said in Ecclesiastes 43 [32], 'Glorify the Lord as much as you are able, yet he will still far exceed' [what you are able].

[16]   Ibid., q. 2, a. 1, ad 7. To the seventh objection it is to be said that God is infinitely distant from creatures, and no creature is moved to God so as to be the equal of God, either in what it receives from God or in what it knows of God. From this it follows that because God is infinitely distant from a creature, God cannot be the terminus of the motion of a creature. And yet, every creature is moved to this: that the creature may be assimilated to God, more and more, *insofar as this is possible*. And it is in this way that the human mind ought to always be moved more and more to knowledge of God, according to the mode of the human mind. And thus it is that Hilary [*De Trinitate* II, 10] says, 'He who in pious spirit undertakes the infinite, even though he can not attain it, nevertheless profits by advancing' [emphasis added].

[17]   Ibid., q. 6, a. 3, resp. The light of divine revelation comes to us adapted to our condition, as Dionysius says [*Celestial Hierarchy* 1, n. 2]. Thus although we are elevated by revelation to know *something* of which we would otherwise be ignorant, *revelation does not elevate us to any other mode of knowledge than by way of sensible things* [emphasis added].

On Aquinas' Intention: The Design of the Finished Expositio

Aquinas' unfinished *Expositio* of the *De Trinitate* actually treated only the "Prologue" and Sections I and II of Boethius' work. And thus one may estimate that Aquinas' *Expositio* was much less than half-finished, even though there are themes from all six sections of the Boethian Tractate which are addressed by Aquinas in his six Questions. But it is incorrect to consider Aquinas' *Expositio* as finished.[18] It may have been left unfinished due to the exceptional difficulties of *agnosia* presented in the Tractate itself, and because of the already full schedule of Aquinas, which left little time for projects not associated with his university and other duties.

Aquinas did actually treat some themes of Boethius' Section III very briefly in his analysis of number and plurality in God (Q. 4). But, as has already been noted, this is due to the fact that Section I of Boethius' Tractate introduces the question of number, plurality, and otherness, and then these themes are returned to in more detail in Section III. What Boethius establishes in Section II is that there is no real diversity in the Trinity by means of genus, species, or number. There cannot be "three" in the Trinity in the natural sense of numerical difference based on accidents such as "place." Indeed, in the natural order of sensible realities, the whole notion of "number" is based on distinctions which cannot apply to the Trinity. One may anticipate that had Aquinas' finished his *Expositio* of Sections III-VI of Boethius' work, he would have addressed the following, very difficult themes:

1) There is, for finite human understanding, no intelligible difference of plurality or number in the Trinity, for the divine Persons are One in Essence.

2) This makes all predication of terms of the particular divine Persons fundamentally impossible to understand, for to understand such terms as "Father," "Son," and "Holy Spirit" would be to understand predicates which refer to the same Essence, but in manners which are "not Identical," and these manners of "non-Identity" are not based on accidents, or on Essence. The only basis of non-Identity is a notion of something like distinct "Subjects," or "Persons," based on the impossible-to-comprehend definition of a Trinitarian Relation as "the Relation of an Identical to an Identical."

3) Since God is beyond all substantial and accidental predication, as God is supersubstantial, no predications adequately apply to God, and God cannot be treated as a "subject" in the sense of a substance which can be known, or in the sense of a substance which has accidents.

---

[18]   This is the impression given by Brennan, complete with a chart attempting to show how all the Boethian themes were actually addressed in Aquinas' six questions, in the "Introduction" to her translation, *The Trinity and the Unicity of the Intellect by Saint Thomas Aquinas* (St. Louis and London: Herder, 1946).

4) When Relation is predicated of God, it does not imply an otherness of Substance or Essence, but something which ultimately can hardly be understood, i.e., only an "otherness" of "Persons" who are Identical Essentially; and yet it is *only* the notion of "Relation" which can try to account for the Trinity of Persons, as "Relations of Identicals."

5) Ultimately, human nature cannot reach beyond the limits of its understanding, and even faith-filled theological attempts to penetrate the mystery of the Trinity end more in a posture of prayerful *agnosia* than of academic victory.

These themes would have been addressed, so it is anticipated, if Aquinas had finished the *Expositio*. One might hope that Aquinas would have addressed the fundamental theme of the ultimate relationship between more Neoplatonic and more Aristotelian approaches to the nature of revelation and the *lumen fidei*, but the indications are that either he was not actually aware of the dialectical interplays in his own positions, or he chose not to surface this underlying structure.

Following the unfinished *Expositio*, Aquinas never again undertook an explicit synthesis of method and Trinity as such. His final, major statement in "The Treatise on the Trinity" in the *Summa Theologiae* does not itself provide any explicit methodological reflections, and it follows only the exceptionally brief and simplified Question 1 of the Prima Pars on the status and method of theology.

Concluding Reflections

Although much has been explored, one may well ask what the present study of Aquinas' *Expositio* of the *De Trinitate* of Boethius has been able to grasp of the Mystery of the Triune God. One must say that what can be grasped of the infinite Mystery by finite theology remains almost nothing.

Theology can grasp some aspects of what God at least must be, and what the relationships of the human person in community and history to the Triune God must at least entail. Some theological models can be found to be inappropriate. But it has been a concern of the present investigation to show that if one follows Aquinas' methodology, one can say almost nothing about the Mystery Itself. One does not judge the Mystery in theology, although one may judge ways of articulating It. Theology itself proceeds from the prior assent of faith, and seeks limited understanding, sapiential savoring, and mystical nourishment. The drive of reason to grasp and accurately classify is subsumed under a more powerful cleaving to the Mystery, which In-Itself remains absolutely impenetrable by theological language. As Aquinas himself stated it:

Humana igitur ratio ad cognoscendum fidei veritatem, quae solum videntibus divinam substantiam potest esse notissima, ita se habet quod ad eam potest aliquas verisimilitudines colligere, quae tamen non sufficiunt ad hoc quod praedicta veritas quasi demonstrative vel per se intellecta comprehendatur. Utile tamen est ut in huismodi rationibus, quantumcumque debilibus, se mens humana exerceat, dummodo desit comprehendendi vel demonstrandi praesumptio: quia de rebus altissimis etiam parva et debili consideratione aliquid posse inspicere iucundissimum est, ut ex dictis apparet.

Cui quidem sententiae auctoritas Hilarii concordat, qui sic dicit in libro de Trin., loquens de huismodi veritate: 'Haec credendo incipe, procurre, persiste: etsi non perventurum sciam, gratulabor tamen profecturum. Qui enim pie infinita prosequitur, etsi non contingat aliquando, semper tamen proficiet prodeundo. Sed ne te inferas in illud secretum, et arcano interminabilis nativitatis non te immergas, summam intelligentiae comprehendere praesumens: sed intellige incomprehensibilia esse.'[19]

Does this mean that a participationist-transcendental-analogical attempt at reasonable, *ex convenientia* theological understanding of the Trinity is a failure in all respects?

On the contrary, in attempting to conceptualize the mystery, the ultimate failure of theology brings out in full the inaccessible height of the mystery. Thomas Aquinas does not climb the mountain in order to have its peak under his feet. He only climbs the hills round the mountain and from these he looks up to the unapproachable clouded peak and he kneels down in the only possible attitude of faith: 'adoro te devote, latens deitas.'[20]

---

[19]   Aquinas, *Summa Contra Gentiles*, Book I, Chapter 8 (Leonine edition). Human reason is related to the knowledge of the truth of faith, a truth which can be most evident only to those who see the divine substance, in such a way that it can gather certain likenesses of it, but these likenesses are not sufficient so that the truth of faith may be comprehended as if it were in some way demonstrated or intellectually comprehended per se. Yet it is useful for human reason to be engaged in such inquiry based on similitudes, however weak and insufficient they may be, provided only that there be present no presumption to comprehend or demonstrate. For to be able to see something of the loftiest realities, however weak and debilitated the sight may be, is, as our previous remarks indicate, a cause of the greatest joy.

The testimony of Hilary agrees with this. Speaking of this same truth, he writes as follows in his *De Trinitate* [II, 10, ii.]: 'Enter these truths by believing, press forward, persevere. And though I may know that you will not arrive at an end, yet I will congratulate you in your progress. For though he who pursues the infinite with reverence will never finally reach the end, yet he will always progress by pressing onward. But do not intrude yourself into the divine secret, do not, presuming to comprehend the sum total of intelligence, plunge yourself into the mystery of the unending nativity; rather, understand that these things are incomprehensible.'

[The translation here is a modification of A. Pegis, *Summa Contra Gentiles*, Book I (Notre Dame: University of Notre Dame Press, 1975), p. 76. This text of Hilary is also cited by Aquinas more briefly in the *Expositio Super Librum Boethii De Trinitate* in q. 2, a. 1, resp. and ad 7.]

[20]   J. Walgrave, "The Use of Philosophy in the Theology of Thomas Aquinas," *Selected Writings*, ed. De Schrijver and Kelly, Bibliotheca Ephemeridum Theologicarum Lovaniensium LVII (Leuven: University Press, 1982), p. 15.

The failure of its conceptualizing attempts is the ultimate dialectical moment in which theology finds itself to be most authentic. Aware of its own finite limits, theology yields itself in patient, powerless, waiting in prayer for the experiential gift of divine wisdom. It is this attitude which Aquinas expressed in his mature years, in his eloquent *Commentary on the Gospel of John*. In considering the invitation of Christ in that Gospel, Aquinas reflected on it in terms of the Indwelling of the Trinity:

> Mystice autem dicit *Venite, et videte* quia habitatio Dei, sive gloriae, sive gratiae, agnosci non potest nisi per experientiam; nam verbis explicari non potest ... .[21]

Theological knowledge and understanding of the Trinity, whether in terms of grace and the Indwelling, or simply in terms of theological articulation of the Mystery of the Trinity as such, is more by way of "suffering the divine" than by way of conceptual articulation in language.

There is a profound and sublime paradox in the theology of Aquinas. For one is quite hard-pressed to find any theologian in history so emphatically committed to the origin of all truth in the One God, and so vigorously confident that the *lumen fidei* can enrich, guide, transform, and intensify on a new level the entire range of natural reason. Yet, on the other hand, one would be equally hard-pressed to find any theologian in history so radically aware of the infinite distance between God and creature, and so utterly insistent that the Essence of the Triune God remains absolutely shrouded in darkness during the sojourn *in via*. In a parallel manner, the sheer intellectual genius of Aquinas could attempt, under the influence of Boethius, to synthesize Aristotelian and Augustinian traditions within an architectonic whose astounding precision is a monument to the logical clarity of which the human mind is capable. And yet, this same Aquinas is the man whose languor in ardent love for God often left him weeping in prayer, unable to speak, and ultimately defeated.

One is lead, with Aquinas, to consider Jacob's struggle with God.

> 'Nequoquam Jacob appelabitur nomen tuum, sed Israel. Quia si contra Deum fortis fuisti,' per violentiam scilicet detentivarum precum et importunarum pulsationum cum Deo pugnando, ejusque rigorem superando, sive flectendo ... . 'Cur quaeris nomen meum, quod est mirabile?' Sensus potest esse, quod hoc dico, mirabile est nomen ejus: vel quod nomen suum est mirabile, quod non est nobis comprehensibile.[22]

---

[21]   Aquinas, *Super Evangelium S. Ioannis*, I, lect. 15, 5. Mystically he says *Come, and see* because God's indwelling, whether by glory or by grace, cannot be known except by experiencing it: it cannot be explained in words ... .

[22]   Aquinas, *In Gen.*, cap. 32 (Vivès edition). 'No longer will you be called Jacob, but Israel. For if you have placed your strength against God,' by means of violence, that is, he grasped God and fought with God, neither overcoming the other, neither yielding ... . 'And you ask my name,

Toute une nuit, ils s'affrontèrent, muscles tenus, sans que l'un ou l'autre cédassent; au petit matin, l'ange disparut, laissant apparemment le terrain à son partenaire; mais Jacob ressentit alors une douleur vive à la cuisse: il restait blessé et claudicant. Ainsi le théologien affronte le mystère, au niveau duquel Dieu l'a porté; il est tendu, comme arc-bouté à ses expressions humaines; il en saisit les objects à bras-le-corps; il semble même s'en rendre maitre: mais il éprouve alors une faiblesse douloureuse et délectable à la fois, car d'être ainsi vaincu est le gage, en vérité, de son divin combat.[23]

---

which is marvelous?' The sense of this can be that here it is said that his name is marvelous, or that his name is marvelous in that is is not comprehensible for us.

[23]   M.-D. Chenu, *La théologie est-elle une science?* Je sais, je crois, vol. 2. (Paris: Libraire Arthème Fayard, 1957), pp. 47-48. The whole night they wrestled, muscles straining, neither yielding; but at daybreak the angel disappeared, apparently leaving the field clear to his adversary. But Jacob then felt a violent pain in his thigh. He was left wounded and limping. It is thus that the theologian grapples with the mystery when God brings him face to face with it. He is taut, like a bent bow, grappling with human language; he struggles like a wrestler; he even seems to win the mastery. But then he feels a weakness, a weakness at once painful and delicious, for to be thus defeated is in fact the proof that his combat was divine.

BIBLIOGRAPHY

Anderson, J. F. *Reflections on the Analogy of Being.* The Hague: Martinus Nijhoff, 1967.
Bardy, G. *Saint Augustin: L'homme et l'oeuvre.* 6th ed. Paris: Desclée de Brouwer, 1946.
Bark, W. "Boethius' Fourth Tractate, The So-Called 'De fide catholica.'" *Harvard Theological Review* 39 (1946), 55-69.
—. "The Legend of Boethius' Martyrdom." *Speculum* 21 (1946), 312-317.
—. "Theoderic vs. Boethius: Vindication and Apology." *American Historical Review* 49 (1944), 410-426.
Barth, K. *Die protestantische Theologie im 19. Jahrhundert: Ihre Vorgeschichte und ihre Geschichte.* Zollikon-Zürich: Evangelischer Verlag, 1952.
—. *Protestant Theology in the Nineteenth Century: Its Background and History.* Trans. Bowden, with some chapters trans. Cozens and rev. by the editorial staff of SCM Press. London: SCM Press, 1972.
Bobrinskoy, B. *Le mystère de la Trinité: cours de théologie orthodoxe.* Paris: Cerf, 1986.
Boethius. *Opera.* Corpus Christianorum, Series Latina. Vol. 94. Ed. L. Bieler. Turnholt: Brepols, 1957.
—. *Theological Tractates.* Ed. and trans. H. Stewart, E. Rand, and S. Tester, Loeb Classical Library, Latin. Vol. 74. Cambridge, MA: Harvard University Press, 1973.
—. *Die theologischen Traktaten.* Ed. and trans. M. Elsasser. Hamburg: Meiner, 1988.
Boff, C. *Theology and Praxis: Epistemological Foundations.* Maryknoll, N.Y.: Orbis, 1987.
Bonnefroy, J.-F. "La théologie comme science et l'explication de la foi selon saint Thomas d'Aquin." *Ephemerides Theologicae Louvanienses* 14 (1937), 421-446.
Boyer, B. and R. McKeon. *Peter Abailard.* Chicago: University of Chicago Press, 1976.
Bracken, J. *The Triune God: Persons, Process, and Community.* Lanham, MD: University Press of America, 1985.
Brown, D. *The Divine Trinity.* La Salla, Ill.: Open Court, 1985.
Cassiodorus. *Opera.* Corpus Christianorum, Series Latina. Vol. 96. Ed. A. Fridh and J. Halporn. Turnhout: Brepols, 1973.
Chadwick, H. "The Authenticity of Boethius' Fourth Tractate 'De fide catholica.'" *Journal of Theological Studies* 31 (1980), 551-556.
—. *Boethius: The Consolations of Music, Logic, Theology, and Philosophy.* Oxford: Clarendon Press, 1981.
Chenu, M.-D. "La date du commentaire de saint Thomas sur le De Trinitate de Boèce." *Les sciences philosophiques et théologiques* 30 (1941/1942), 432-434.
—. *La théologie comme science au XIIIe siècle.* Paris: Desclée, 1957.
—. *La théologie est-elle une science?* Je sais, je crois. Vol. 2. Paris: Libraire Arthème Fayard, 1957.
Cobb, J. *A Christian Natural Theology Based on the Thought of Alfred North Whitehead.* London: Lutterworth Press, 1966.
Congar, Y. "Théologie." *Dictionnaire de Théologie Catholique,* XV, 1, cc. 341-502.
—. *A History of Theology.* Trans. Guthrie. Garden City: Doubleday, 1968.
—. *Je crois en l'Esprit Saint.* 3 vols. Paris: Cerf, 1980.
de Contenson, P.-M. "Documents sur les premiéres anneés de la Commission Léonine." *St. Thomas Aquinas 1274-1974: Commemorative Studies.* 2 vols., ed. A. Maurer. Toronto: Pontifical Institute of Mediaeval Studies, 1974, vol. 2, pp. 331-388.
—. "Principles, Methods, and Problems of the Critical Edition of the Works of St. Thomas as Presented in the Leonine Edition." *Tijdschrift voor Philosophie* 36 (1974), 342-364.
Corbin, M. *Le chemin de la théologie chez Thomas d'Aquin.* Paris: Beauchesne, 1974.
Cousins, E. (ed.) *Process Theology: Basic Writings.* New York: Newman Press, 1971.

Crämer-Rugenberg, I. *Die Substanzmetaphysik des Boethius in den Opuscula sacra*. Ph.D. dissertation, University of Cologne, 1967.

Daniélou, J. *La Trinité et le mystere de l'existence*. Bruges: Desclée de Brouwer, 1968.

—. *God's Life in Us*. Trans. Leggat. Denville, N.J.: Dimension Books, 1969.

Decker, B. "Prolegomena." *Sancti Thomae de Aquino Expositio Super Librum Boethii De Trinitate*. Ed. Decker. Leiden: Brill, 1955, repr. with corrections, 1959, 1965.

Degl' Innocenti, U. "Il pensiero di san Tommaso sul principio d'individuazione." *Divus Thomas* (Piacenza) 45 (1942), 35-81.

Denifle, H. and E. Châtelain (eds.) *Chartularium Universitatis Parisiensis*. Vol. 1. Paris: Delalain, 1889.

Dondaine, A. *Les secrétaires de s. Thomas*. 2 vols. Rome: Leonine Commission, 1956.

Elders, L. *Faith and Science: An Introduction to St. Thomas' 'Expositio in Boethii De Trinitate.'* Studia Universitatis S. Thomae in Urbe. Rome: Herder, 1974.

Eschmann, I. "A Catalogue of St. Thomas' Works: Bibliographical Notes." In E. Gilson, *The Christian Philosophy of St. Thomas Aquinas*. New York: Random House, 1956, pp. 381-439.

Evans, G. "More Geometrico: The Place of the Axiomatic Method in the Twelfth-Century Commentaries on Boethius' Opuscula Sacra." *Archives Internationales d'histoire des sciences* 27 (1977) 207-221.

Fabro, C. "The Intensive Hermeneutics of Thomistic Philosophy: The Notion of Participation." *The Review of Metaphysics* 27 (1974), 449-491.

—. *La nozione metafisica di participazione secondo S. Tommaso d'Aquino*. Milano: Soc. Ed. Vita e Pensiero, 1939; 2nd ed. Torino: Soc. Ed. Internazionale, 1950, 3rd ed. 1963.

—. *Partecipazione e causalità*. Torino: Soc. Ed. Internazionale, 1961.

—. *Participation et causalité selon s. Thomas d'Aquin*. Louvain: Publications Universitaires, 1961.

Fransen, P. *The New Life of Grace*. Trans. DuPont, Foreword by J. MacQuarrie. London: Geoffrey Chapman, 1969.

Garrigou-Lagrange, R. *De Deo Uno: Commentarium in Primam Partem S. Thomae*. Paris: Desclée de Brouwer et Cie, 1938.

Geiger, L.-B. *La participation dans la philosophie de s. Thomas d'Aquin*. Paris: Vrin, 1942, 2nd ed. 1952.

—. "Abstraction et séparation d'après saint Thomas." *Revue des sciences philosophiques et théologiques* 31 (1947), 3-40.

Gibson, M. "The Opuscula Sacra in the Middle Ages." *Boethius: His Life, Thought and Influence*. Ed. M. Gibson. Oxford: Basil Blackwell, 1981, pp. 214-234.

Gils, P.-M. "L'édition Decker du 'In Boethium de Trinitate' et les autographs de s. Thomas d'Aquin." *Scriptorium* 10 (1956) 111-120.

—. [Notes on the 1959 edition.] *Bulletin thomiste* 11 (1960-1961) 41-44.

Gilson, E. *The Christian Philosophy of St. Thomas Aquinas*. New York: Random House, 1956.

Glorie, F. "Augustinus, 'De Trinitate': Fontes - Chronologia." *Sacris Erudiri* 16 (1965), 203-255.

Gonzalez, A. *Ser y participación. Estudio sobre la cuarta via de Tomás de Aquino*. Pamplona: Eunsa, 1979.

Gonzales de Cardedal, O. *Teologia y Antropologia, el hombre 'imagen de Dios' en el pensamiento de Santo Tomás*. Estudios de teologia 1. Madrid: Editorial Moneda y Credito, 1967.

Grabmann, M. *Die theologische Erkenntnis- und Einleitungslehre des hl. Thomas von Aquin auf Grund seiner Schrift 'In Boethium de Trinitate,' im Zusammenhang der Scholastik des 13. und beginnenden 14. Jahrhunderts dargestellt*. Freiburg: Paulusverlag, 1948.

—. *Die Werke des hl. Thomas von Aquin*. Münster: Aschendorff, 1931.

Gracia, J. *Introduction to the Problem of Individuation in the Early Middle Ages*. Washington, D.C.: The Catholic University of America Press, 1984.

Hadot, P. "La distinction de l'être et de l'étant dans le 'De Hebdomadibus' de Boèce." *Miscellanea Mediaevalia*. Ed. P. Wilpert. Berlin: Walter De Gruyter, 1963, pp. 147-153.

Hall, D. "Immediacy and Mediation in Aquinas: 'In I Sent.,' Q. 1, A. 5." *The Thomist* 53 (1989), 31-55.

Hartley, T. *Thomistic Revival and the Modernist Era.* St. Michael's in Toronto Studies in Religion and Theology, Dissertation Series 1. Toronto: Institute of Christian Thought, University of St. Michael's College, 1971.

Häring, N. (ed.) *The Commentaries on Boethius by Gilbert of Poitiers.* Studies and Texts XIII. Toronto: Pontifical Institute of Mediaeval Studies, 1966.

—. (ed.) *The Commentaries on Boethius by Thierry of Chartres and His School.* Toronto: Pontifical Institute of Mediaeval Studies, 1971.

Hendrikx, E. "Le date de composition du 'De Trinitate' de saint Augustin." *L'année théologique augustinienne* 12 (1952), 305-316.

Hill, W. *Knowing the Unknown God.* New York: Philosophical Library, 1971.

—. *Proper Relations to the Indwelling Divine Persons.* Washington, D.C.: The Thomist Press, 1955.

—. *The Three-Personed God: The Trinity as a Mystery of Salvation.* Washington, D.C.: The Catholic University of America Press, 1982.

—. [Review of J. Bracken, *The Triune God.*] *The Thomist* 51 (1987), 172-176.

International Theological Commission. "L'Unité de la foi et le pluralisme théologique." *La Civiltá Cattolica* (5 May 1973); also published in *La documentation catholique* (20 May 1973).

Jüngel, E. *Gottes Sein ist im Werden. Veranwortliche Rede vom Sein Gottes bei Karl Barth: eine Paraphrase.* Tübingen: Mohr, 1965.

—. *The Doctrine of the Trinity: God's Being in Becoming.* Grand Rapids: Eerdmans, 1976.

Kappelmacher, A. "Der schriftstellerische Plan des Boethius." *Wiener Studien* 46 (1929), 215-225.

Kleutgen, J. *Die Theologie der Vorzeit.* 2 vols. Münster: Theissing, 1853, 1854.

—. *Die Philosophie der Vorzeit vertheidigt.* 2nd ed. Innsbruck: Rausch, 1878.

Klinger, I. *Das Prinzip der Individuation bei Thomas von Aquin.* Munsterschwarzach: Vier-Turme, 1964.

Klubertanz, G. *St. Thomas Aquinas on Analogy: A Textual Analysis and Systematic Synthesis.* Chicago: Loyola University Press, 1960.

Klünker, W.-U. "Einführung." *Thomas von Aquin: Über die Trinität: Eine Auslegung der gleichnamigen Schrift des Boethius in Librum Boethii de Trinitate Expositio.* Übersetzung und Erläuterungen von H. Lentz, mit einer Einführung von W.-U. Klünker. Stuttgart: Verlag Freies Geistesleben, 1988.

Küng, H. *Christ sein.* Munich: Piper, 1974.

—. *On Being a Christian.* Trans. Quinn. Garden City: Doubleday, 1976.

LaFont, G. *Structures et méthode dans la Somme Théologique de saint Thomas.* Paris: Desclée de Brouwer, 1960.

Liebeschütz, H. "Boethius and the Legacy of Antiquity." *The Cambridge History of Later Greek and Early Medieval Philosophy.* Ed. A. Armstrong. Cambridge: Cambridge University Press, 1967.

Lonergan, B. *Collection: Papers by Bernard Lonergan.* Ed. F. Crowe. New York: Herder and Herder, 1968.

—. *De Deo Trino.* 2 vols. Rome: Gregorian University Press, 1964.

—. *Divinarum personarum conceptio analogica.* Rome: Gregorian University Press, 1957.

—. *Insight: A Study of Human Understanding.* New York: Philosophical Library, 1957.

—. *Method in Theology.* New York: Herder and Herder, 1972.

—. *Verbum: Word and Idea in Aquinas.* Ed. D. Burrell. Notre Dame: University of Notre Dame Press, 1967.

Lyttkens, H. *The Analogy Between God and the World: An Investigation of Its Background and Interpretation of Its Use by Thomas of Aquino.* Uppsala: Almqvist and Wicksells, 1952.

Mair, J. "The Text of the 'Opuscula Sacra.'" *Boethius: His Life, Thought and Influence.* Ed. M. Gibson. Oxford: Basil Blackwell, 1981, pp. 206-213.

Mandonnet, P. "Introduction." *Quaestiones Disputatae.* Ed. P. Mandonnet. Paris: Lethielleux, 1925.

—. *Des écrits authentique de saint Thomas d'Aquin.* 2nd ed. rev. and corrected, Fribourg: S. Paul, 1910.

Maréchal, J. *Le point de départ de la métaphysique. Leçons sur le développement historique et théorique du problème de la connaissance.* Bruges: Beyaert; Louvain: Museum Lessianum, 4 vols., 1923-26; 3rd ed. Bruxelles: Editions Universelles; Paris: Desclée, 5 vols., 1944ff.

McCool, G. *Catholic Theology in the Nineteenth Century: The Quest for A Unitary Method.* New York: Seabury, 1977.

—. *From Unity to Pluralism: The Internal Evolution of Thomism.* New York: Fordham University Press, 1989.

McInerny, R. *Boethius and Aquinas.* Washington, D.C.: The Catholic University of America Press, 1990.

—. *The Logic of Analogy: An Interpretation of St. Thomas.* The Hague: Martinus Nijhoff, 1961.

—. *Studies in Analogy.* The Hague: Martinus Nijhoff, 1968.

McKinlay, A. "Stylistic Tests and the Chronology of the Works of Boethius." *Harvard Studies in Classical Philology* 18 (1907), 123-156.

McNicholl, A. "On Judging." *The Thomist* 38 (1974), 789-825.

—. "On Judging Existence." *The Thomist* 43 (1979), 507-580.

Merriell, D. *To the Image of the Trinity: A Study in the Development of Aquinas' Teaching.* Studies and Texts, 96. Toronto: Pontifical Institute of Mediaeval Studies, 1990.

Moltmann, J. *Kirche in der Kraft des Geistes: ein Beitrag zur messianischen Ekklesiologie.* Munich: Kaiser, 1975.

—. *The Church in the Power of the Spirit: A Contribution to Messianic Ecclesiology.* Trans. Kohl. London: SCM, 1977.

—. *Trinität und Reich Gottes: zur Gotteslehre.* Munich: Kaiser, 1980.

—. *The Trinity and the Kingdom of God.* Trans. Kohl. London: SCM, 1981.

Mondin, B. *The Principle of Analogy in Protestant and Catholic Theology.* The Hague: Martinus Nijhoff, 1963.

Montagnes, B. *La doctrine de l'analogie de l'être d'après s. Thomas d'Aquin.* Louvain: Publications Universitaires, 1963.

Murphy, C. "All the Pope's Men: Putting Aquinas Together Again." *Harper's* (June 1979), 45-64.

Neumann, S. *Gegenstand und Methode der theoretischen Wissenschaften nach Thomas von Aquin auf Grund der Expositio super librum Boethii de Trinitate.* Münster: Aschendorff, 1965.

Nicolas, J. *Synthèse dogmatique: de la Trinité à la Trinité.* Paris: Beauchesne, 1985.

Niebuhr, H. R. "The Doctrine of the Trinity and the Unity of the Church." *Theology Today* 3 (1946), 371-384.

Nietzsche, F. *Twilight of the Idols and the Antichrist.* Baltimore: Penguin, 1968.

O'Brien, T. "'Sacra Doctrina' Revisited: The Context of Medieval Education." *The Thomist* 41 (1977), 475-509.

O'Donnell, J. [Review of 1973 Loeb Edition of Boethius.] *American Journal of Philology* 98 (1977), 77-79.

—. *Cassiodorus.* Los Angeles: University of California Press, 1978.

Obertello, L. *Boezio: la Consolazione della Filosofia, e gli Opuscoli Teologici.* Milan: Rusconi, 1979.

—. *Severino Boezio.* 2 vols. Genoa: Academia Ligura di Scienze e Lettere, 1974.

Ogden, S. *The Reality of God and Other Essays.* New York: Harper and Row, 1963.

Owens, J. "Aquinas on Knowing Existence." *The Review of Metaphysics* 29 (1976), 670-690.

—. "Metaphysical Separation in Aquinas." *Mediaeval Studies* 34 (1972), 287-306.

Patch, H. "The Beginnings of the Legend of Boethius." *Speculum* 22 (1947), 443-445.

Pelikan, J. *The Christian Tradition: A History of the Development of Doctrine.* Vol. 1: *The Emergence of the Catholic Tradition, 100-600.* Chicago: The University of Chicago Press, 1971.

Persson, P. "Le plan de la Somme théologique et la rapport Ratio-Revelatio." *Revue philosophique de Louvain* (1958), 545-572.

—. *Sacra Doctrina: Reason and Revelation in Aquinas.* Trans. MacKenzie. Philadelphia: Fortress Press, 1970.

Pittenger, N. *Process Thought and Christian Faith.* Welwyn, Herts: Nisbet, 1968.

Preller, V. *Divine Science and the Science of God: A Reformulation of Thomas Aquinas*. Princeton: Princeton University Press, 1967.

Principe, W. *Hugh of Saint-Cher's Theology of the Hypostatic Union*. Studies and Texts XIX. Toronto: Pontifical Institute of Mediaeval Studies, 1970.

de Raeymaeker, L. *Metaphysica Generalis*. 2nd ed. Louvain: Warny, 1935.

—. *De metaphysiek van het zijn*. Antwerpen: Standaard Boekhandel; Nijmegen: Dekker and Van der Vegt, 1944, 2nd ed. 1947.

—. *Philosophie de l'être: Essai de synthèse métaphysique*. Louvain: Institut Supérieur de Philosophie, 1945, 2nd ed. 1947; 3rd ed. Louvain: Editions Nauwelaerts; Paris: Béatrice-Nauwelaerts, 1970.

—. Trans. Ziegelmeyer. *The Philosophy of Being: A Synthesis of Metaphysics*. London and St. Louis: Herder, 1966.

Rahner, K. "Bemerkungen zum dogmatischen Traktat 'De Trinitate.'" *Schriften zur Theologie*, 4. Einsiedeln, Zürich, Köln: Benzinger Verlag, 1960, pp. 103-133.

—. "Remarks on the Dogmatic Treatise 'De Trinitate.'" *Theological Investigations*. Vol. 4. Trans. Smyth. Baltimore: Helicon Press; London: Darton, Longman and Todd, 1966, pp. 77-102

—. "Der dreifaltige Gott als transzendenter Urgrund der Heilsgeschichte." Kapitel 5 in *Mysterium Salutis: Grundriss heilsgeschichtlicher Dogmatik*, 2. Ed. Feiner and Löhrer. Einsiedeln, Zürich, Köln: Benzinger Verlag, 1967, pp. 317-401.

—. *The Trinity*. Trans. Donceel. New York: Herder and Herder, 1970.

—. *Geist in Welt. Zur Metaphysik der endlichen Erkenntis bei Thomas von Aquin*. Innsbruck-Leipzig: Rausch, 1939; 2nd ed., rev. by J. Metz, Munich: Kösel-Verlag, 1957.

—. *Spirit in the World*. Trans. of 2nd ed. by Dych. New York: Herder and Herder, 1968.

—. "Zur scholastischen Begrifflichkeit der ungeschaffenen Gnade." *Schriften zur Theologie*, 1. Einsiedeln, Zürich, Köln: Benzinger Verlag, 1954, pp. 347-375.

—. "Some Implications of the Scholastic Concept of Uncreated Grace." *Theological Investigations*. Vol. 1. Trans. Ernst. Baltimore: Helicon Press, 1961, pp. 319-346.

Rand, E. *The Founders of the Middle Ages*. Cambridge: Harvard University Press, 1928.

Sala, G. *Das Apriori in der menschlichen Erkenntnis: eine Studie über Kants Kritik der reinen Vernunft und Lonergans Insight*. Meisenheim am Glan: Hain, 1971.

Sanchez Sorondo, M. *La gracia como participación de la naturaleza divina*. Buenos Aires-Letran-Salamanca: Universidades Pontificias, 1979.

Schillebeeckx, E. *Revelation and Theology*. Vol. 1 New York: Sheed and Ward, 1967.

Schindler, A. *Wort und Analogie in Augustins Trinitätslehre*. Tübingen: Mohr, 1965.

Schmidt, R. "L'Emploi de la séparation en métaphysique." *Revue philosophique de Louvain* 58 (1960), 376-393.

Schrimpf, G. *Die Axiomenschrift des Boethius (de Hebdomadibus) als Philosophisches Lehrbuch des Mittelalters*. Leiden: Brill, 1966.

Schurr, V. *De Trinitätslehre des Boethius im Lichte der 'skythischen Kontroversen,'* Forschungen z. Christlichen Literatur u. Dogmengeschichte XVIII. Paderborn, 1933.

Sciacca, M. "Riflessioni sui principi della metafisica tomista: l'esistenza e l'essenza; la creazione, la partecipazione e l'analogia." *Tommaso d'Aquino nel suo VII Centenario*. 9 vols. Rome: Herder; Naples: d'Auria, 1975-1978. Vol. 3, pp. 18-29.

Synave, P. "La révélation des vérités divines naturelles d'après saint Thomas." *Mélanges Mandonnet: études d'histoire litteraire et doctrinale du moyen âge*. Vol. 1. Paris: Vrin, 1930, pp. 327-365.

—. "Le problème chronologique des questions disputées de s. Thomas d'Aquin." *Revue thomiste* 31 (1926), 156-159.

Tallon, A. "Spirit, Matter, Becoming: Karl Rahner's 'Spirit in the World (Geist in Welt).'" *The Modern Schoolman* 48 (1971), 151-165.

Thomas Aquinas. *Expositio Super Librum Boethii De Trinitate*. Ed. B. Decker. Leiden: Brill, 1955, repr. with corrections, 1959, 1965.

—. *In librum Boethii De Trinitate Quaestiones quinta et sexta*. Ed. P. Wyser. Fribourg and Louvain: Societé philosophique, 1948.

—. *The Division and Methods of the Sciences: Questions V and VI of his Commentary on the 'De Trinitate' of Boethius.* Trans. with Introduction and Notes by A. Maurer. 3rd rev. ed. Toronto: The Pontifical Institute of Mediaeval Studies, 1963; 4th ed. 1986.

—. *Faith, Reason, and Theology: Questions I-IV of his Commentary on the 'De Trinitate' of Boethius.* Trans. with Introduction and Notes by A. Maurer. Medieval Sources In Translation, 32 Toronto: Pontifical Institute of Medieval Studies, 1987.

—. *Summa Contra Gentiles.* Book I. Trans. A. Pegis. Notre Dame: University of Notre Dame Press, 1975.

—. *Summa Theologiae.* Vol. 1: *Christian Theology.* Trans. with Introduction, Notes, Appendices and Glossary by T. Gilby. New York: McGraw-Hill Book Company; London: Eyre and Ode, 1964.

—. *Über die Trinität: Eine Auslegung der gleichnamigen Schrift des Boethius in Librum Boethii de Trinitate Expositio.* Übersetzung und Erläuterungen von H. Lentz, mit einer Einführung von W.-U. Klünker. Stuttgart: Verlag Freies Geistesleben, 1988.

Tracy, D. *Blessed Rage for Order.* New York: Seabury, 1975.

Van Ackeren, G. *Sacra Doctrina: The Subject of the First Question of the Summa Theologica of St. Thomas Aquinas.* Rome: Catholic Book Agency, 1952.

Vos, A. *Aquinas, Calvin and Contemporary Protestant Thought: A Critique of Protestant Views on the Thought of Thomas Aquinas.* Grand Rapids: Eerdmans, 1985.

Wagner, J. "A Study of What Can and Cannot be Determined about 'Separatio' as it is Discussed in the Works of Thomas Aquinas." Ph.D. Dissertation, The Catholic University of America, The School of Philosophy, Studies in Philosophy no. 278, 1979.

Walgrave, J. *Selected Writings.* Ed. De Schrijver and Kelly, Bibliotheca Ephemeridum Theologicarum Lovaniensium LVII. Leuven: University Press, 1982.

Weidemann, H. *Metaphysik und Sprache. Eine sprachphilosophische Untersuchung zu Thomas von Aquin und Aristoteles.* Freiburg-Munich: Karl Alber, 1975.

Weisheipl, J. *Friar Thomas d'Aquino: His Life, Thought, and Work.* Garden City: Doubleday, 1974.

—. "The Meaning of 'Sacra Doctrina' in 'Summa Theologiae' I, q. 1." *The Thomist* 38 (1974), 49-80.

Williams, D. *The Spirit and Forms of Love.* New York: Harper and Row, 1968.

Wippel, J. "Metaphysics and 'Separatio' in Thomas Aquinas." *The Review of Metaphysics* 31 (1978), 431-470.

—. *Metaphysical Themes in Thomas Aquinas.* Washington, D.C.: The Catholic University of America Press, 1984.

—. "Thomas Aquinas on the Distinction and Derivation of the Many from the One: A Dialectic between Being and Nonbeing." *The Review of Metaphysics* 38 (1985), 563-590.

Zeiller, J. "Les églises ariennes de Rome à l'époque de la domination gothique." *Mélanges de l'école française de Rome* 24 (1905), 127-146.

INDEX OF AUTHORS

STUDIEN UND TEXTE
ZUR GEISTESGESCHICHTE
DES MITTELALTERS

HERAUSGEGEBEN VON

DR. ALBERT ZIMMERMAN

3. Koch, J. (Hrsg.). *Humanismus, Mystik und Kunst in der Welt des Mittelalters.* 2nd. impr. 1959. *reprint under consideration*
4. Thomas Aquinas, *Expositio super Librum Boethii De trinitate.* Ad fidem codicis autographi nec non ceterorum codicum manu scriptorum recensuit B. Decker. Editio photomechanice iterata 1965. ISBN 90 04 02173 6
5. Koch, J. (Hrsg.). *Artes liberales.* Von der antiken Bildung zur Wissenschaft der Mittelalters. Repr. 1976. ISBN 90 04 04738 7
6. Meuthen. E. *Kirche und Heilsgeschichte bei Gerhoh von Reichersberg.* 1959. ISBN 90 04 02174 4
7. Nothdurft, K.-D. *Studien zum Einfluss Senecas auf die Philosophie und Theologie des Zwölften Jahrhunderts.* 1963. ISBN 90 04 02175 2
9. Zimmerman, A. (Hrsg.). *Verzeichnis ungedruckter Kommentare zur Metaphysik und Physik des Aristoteles aus der Zeit von etwa 1250-1350.* Band I. 1971. ISBN 90 04 02177 9
10. McCarthy, J.M. *Humanistic emphases in the educational thought of Vincent of Beauvais.* 1976. ISBN 90 04 04375 6
11. William of Doncaster. *Explicatio Aphorismatum Philosophicorum.* Edited with annotations by O. Weijers. 1976. ISBN 90 04 04403 5
12. Pseudo-Boèce. *De Disciplina Scolarium.* Édition critique, introduction et notes par O. Weijers. 1976. ISBN 90 04 04768 9
13. Jacobi, K. *Die Modalbegriffe in den logischen Schriften des Wilhelm von Shyreswood und in anderen Kompendien des 12. und 13. Jahrhunderts.* Funktionsbestimmung und Gebrauch in der logischen Analyse. 1980. ISBN 90 04 06048 0
14. Weijers, O. (éd.). *Les questions de Craton et leurs commentaires.* Édition critique. 1981. ISBN 90 04 06340 4
15. Hermann of Carinthia. *De Essentiis.* A critical edition with translation and commentary by Ch. Burnett. 1982. ISBN 90 04 06534 2
16. Goddu, A. *The physics of William of Ockham.* 1984. ISBN 90 04 06912 7
17. John of Salisbury. *Entheticus Maior and Minor.* Edited by J. van Laarhoven. 1987. 3 vols. 1 Introduction, texts, translations; 2. Commentaries and notes; 3. Bibliography, Dutch translations, indexes. ISBN 90 04 07811 8
18. Richard Brinkley. *Theory of sentential reference.* Edited and translated with introduction and notes by M.J. Fitzgerald. 1987. ISBN 90 04 08430 4
19. Alfred of Sareshel. *Commentary on the Metheora of Aristotle.* Critical edition, introduction and notes by J.K. Otte. 1988 ISBN 90 04 08453 3
20. Roger Bacon. *Compendium of the study of theology.* Edition and translation with introduction and notes by T.S. Maloney. 1988. ISBN 90 04 08510 6
21. Aertsen, J.A. *Nature and creature.* Thomas Aquinas's way of thought. 1988 ISBN 90 04 08451 7
22. Tachau, K.H. *Vision and certitude in the age of Ockham.* Optics, epistemology and the foundations of semantics 1250-1345. 1988. ISBN 90 04 08552 1
23. Frakes, J.C. *The fate of fortune in the Early Middle Ages.* The Boethian tradition. 1988. ISBN 90 04 08544 0

24. MURALT, A. DE. *L'enjeu de la philosophie médiévale*. Études thomistes, scotistes, occamiennes et grégoriennes. 1991. ISBN 90 04 09254 4

25. LIVESEY, S.J. *Theology and science in the fourteenth century*. Three questions on the unity and subalternation of the sciences from John of Reading's Commentary on the *Sentences*. Introduction and critical edition. 1989. ISBN 90 04 09023 1

26. ELDERS, L.J. *The philosophical theology of St. Thomas Aquinas*. 1990. ISBN 90 04 09156 4

27. WISSINK, J.B. (ed.). *The eternity of the world in the thought of Thomas Aquinas and his contemporaries*. 1990. ISBN 90 04 09183 1

28. SCHNEIDER, N. *Die Kosmologie des Franciscus de Marchia*. Texte, Quellen und Untersuchungen zur Naturphilosophie des 14. Jahrhunderts. 1991. ISBN 90 04 09280 3

29. LANGHOLM, O. *Economics in the Medieval Schools*. Wealth, Exchange, Value, Money and Usury according to the Paris Theological Tradition 1200-1350. 1992. ISBN 90 04 09422 9

30. RIJK, L.M. DE. *Peter of Spain (Petrus Hispanus Portugalensis): Syncategoreumata*. First Critical Edition with an Introduction and Indexes. With an English Translation by JOKE SPRUYT. 1992. ISBN 90 04 09434 2

31. RESNICK, I.M. *Divine Power and Possibility in St. Peter Damian's* De Divina Omnipotentia. 1992. ISBN 90 04 09572 1

32. O'ROURKE, F. *Pseudo-Dionysius and the Metaphysics of Aquinas*. 1992. ISBN 90 04 09466 0

33. HALL, D.C. *The Trinity*. An Analysis of St. Thomas Aquinas' *Expositio* of the *De Trinitate* of Boethius. 1992. ISBN 90 04 09631 0